IF IT'S NORMAL THEN IT'S PROBABLY NOT FUN

Moopliss

Battle Press

SATELLITE BEACH, FL

If It's Normal Then It's Probably Not Fun

Copyright © 2021 by Matthew Statson

Front cover art by Salome Sahin

Battle Press Books may be ordered through booksellers or by contacting:

Battle Press
1-919-218-4039
steve@battlepress.media

ISBN: 978-1-5136-8539-7 (SC)

ISBN: 978-1-5136-8540-3 (eBook)

First Edition.

The stories and thoughts of Matthew as he explains what he has learned from playing this multiplayer experience within the last 24 years of his life.

Contents

Level 25 On This Floating Rock

People who look like they have their life together are just extremely good at pretending they know what they are doing. Think about it, as people we have no idea what will happen tomorrow. For all we know a meteorite could hit our little floating planet and everything we have built up or created will be gone. It's a little depressing to think about, but the chances of another big rock hitting our big rock that we live on is very unlikely. Perhaps something more possible that will happen is we will die from a natural disaster, get in a car accident, or maybe something crazy will happen, such as a mutant virus spreads like wildfire and eventually hits your poor human body and destroys you from the inside. Yikes. All of these plausible outcomes could happen to any of us. What I'm saying is, as humans we are incredibly fragile lifeforms, and the fact we are alive and breathing is truly crazy to think about.

This is why my parents believe in god. They think it's insane that life exists in the middle of the cosmos on this water rich blue planet with some grass on it for us all to live on and not drown. My dad said that it's impossible that a giant explosion happened years ago and that somebody from up above had to have created this whole universe. I have enough bickering about god later on in this book, but I'll hold my tongue until a later date. I don't know the answer as to why we are alive, in fact I don't know much about anything. I keep trying to remind myself that I'm just an intelligent monkey who somehow has made it this far in my life, and that it's incredible I am able to communicate with others and tell my stories about what I learned. You name the topic and it's probably covered in this book.

For one thing I'm getting older. In this book, I discuss being an adult. I made it to level 25 on this floating rock. Now I've entered the middle of my twenties. Is that ancient? Anywho, it's safe to say I'm no longer a kid, which is insane because even though I'm in my mid-twenties, I think I act like a nine-year-old. If I was able to stop going to work, go outside and swing sticks at trees pretending for them to be lightsabers and then to head inside at night and play video games with family or friends, I'd do that for a long time. Sadly I need to be able to eat food and have a roof over my head to protect me from the elements, which is why I need to act like an adult and chase money. That section of the book is all about discussing how stupid society is and the fact that we all live our lives with certain opportunities that can come our way depending on how much paper is inside our bank account. All you need to know for now is that I fucking despise the fact that I will probably spend a large portion of my life trying to collect money so that I don't starve. Long story short, I'm thankful you bought my book.

Another topic I cover is love, ahh yes. That thing there seems to be many songs, films, and even art that is made to discuss and share our human experience of feeling love. As a person, I love all sorts of things, but the one thing that is special about love is that we get to love other humans. Once in love, we can experience all sorts of fun things that being in love can do. The other person will care for you if you need help.

They'll feed you, look after you if you get sick, talk to you if you are upset or sad about things in your life, and maybe if you are in a relationship, you'll be able to be intimate with this person. I think it's safe to say that there are some aspects of being in love that are quite pleasant. However, love is scary if you think about it, because in order to love another person, we have to set ourselves up to be vulnerable. Being in this state is daunting, because you have no idea if the person will backstab and betray you down the line, which is a thing that can dramatically affect you for the rest of your little human life. Believe it or not, I cover both of these topics. In one chapter I talk about the kind of love that hits you in a good way with how it warms your heart and makes you smile from cheek to cheek with the pure thought of this person that you adore. In another chapter, I discuss how I sadly get fucked up by some girl who pulls the rug out from under my feet, which leads to me developing trust issues with other humans for a couple years, and sets me on a path to find dopamine with something not so good to rely on. What is that thing I started taking to put myself in a happy mood?

Drugs, which happens to be another chapter I wrote about in this book. Specifically marijuana, edibles, shrooms, and LSD. Hey kids, it's your friendly neighborhood author here to remind you not to take drugs. To be honest, drugs make you feel kinda funky, but in the long run, if you are not careful, they can distract you from your goals and send you to some pretty scary experiences. The very first chapter of this book will be a story on how I truly made a grave mistake of taking two laced LSD tabs in Manhattan. I figured the story of me almost dying is good enough for you to stick around and keep reading this book. Drugs entered my life when I got incredibly depressed, it was the thing I ran to as a young adult that I thought would fill this void inside myself and give me a little bit of happiness. Regardless of what I experienced during my trips and how it changed my mindset, it's sad to say that having a drug addiction is not fun, and the one I did have, which was with marijuana edibles, led me down a path that was difficult and hard to handle. I hurt a lot of people along the way and lost a lot of time in my life during the process, but that's okay, sometimes life is about learning from the new things you try.

One new thing I did in my life was moving to Europe. Could you believe that I moved to this other continent to be with a girl I had met on Tinder? Want to know something even more insane? I moved days before a global pandemic hit. Imagine me being in a brand new country, that even if I wanted to get out, I had no way of doing so because all the airports were closed, and yet I didn't even speak the language or have a job yet. Not gonna lie, it was one of the strangest parts I've witnessed in my life. Felt like a glitch in the simulation with how quiet it was when everyone was in quarantine. I tried my best to describe it with words, but in all honesty, it's the kind of thing that you had to be there to experience it. Luckily, it hit worldwide, so if you were alive during 2020 with a consciousness developed that could understand what was happening around your given surroundings, then you probably experienced this catastrophic event as well. Did I know how to react during this time? No.

Was I slightly traumatic with everything happening? Yes. Perhaps I came out of the pandemic trusting the government more? No. Would I really spend a majority of my time playing video games while under lockdown? Yes.

Oh, I know what you want to read. Perhaps you'll jump straight to the part where I replicate people or other characters from video games, movies or real life. Some people know this kind of aspect of copying by having experience of dressing up on Halloween or perhaps you cosplay as one of your favorite superhero characters, but I am somebody who can mimic others just by studying footage and content about them online. This process started when I was acting in high school, but soon grew into my regular day life when I was unable to find plays or musicals to be cast in. Sounds bizarre, but I did it as a coping mechanism to get through tough or strange parts of my life. It might not make any sense to you, but because I did it for several years, I think it deserves a spot in this book. From Justin Bieber, Adam Driver, video game characters and even a YouTuber on the internet, I copied and mimicked bits and pieces of all these people within my life. Perhaps if you feel super inspired by me, you can carry on the practice and mimic me. Just kidding, don't do that. It's kinda weird and strange, people might stare at you and judge you for what you are doing. Believe me, you'll get used to it as time goes on.

speaking of time, it's something that isn't endless and doesn't last forever. i could give you a brief overview of all the other sections that are in this book, but you should just sit down and digest each chapter as it comes along. i wrote about all the things i have previously mentioned and other random shit i felt like i needed to say. basically, i wanted to write everything that has ever happened to me within the past 24 years of my life that felt to be important in my eyes. all my experiences that affected me and lead me to this place in my life are inside this book. nothing is organized either, so this may not be like a regular book to you, but i don't care. do me a favor, learn from my mistakes and hopefully educate yourself on a thing or two. just remember i'm simply another human and i'm probably not the smartest or brightest person to walk on this planet. i don't want to be a role model in your life. i'm just matthew, a person who decided to write a bunch of words onto some pages about his life that hopefully others can read and at least be entertained by it. doesn't matter if the stuff i write about embarrasses me because it's not like my book will be on the earth forever. one day, far in the future, our sun will explode and our earth will no longer be here. f in the chat for that future event. until then, i'm going to keep living my life and not overthink things, in fact i might write this whole paragraph in lowercase letters to prove i don't care so much, you know what yeah, it's all lowercase, even my own name.

One Two One Eight

I find it bizarre that a city with millions of people can make you feel so alone. That's how I felt when I lived in New York City from 2017-2020. Not all the time, but there were times I realized I was just a small living organism in a cement maze that was overcrowded with other dream chasers like myself. It wasn't the worst experience when I was alone, in fact it felt like I was playing a single player adventure game of exploring wherever I wanted to wander, and was able to learn more about myself. One day I remember waking up on April 19th, 2019. Bicycle day. Maybe you don't know what bicycle day is but it's not what you think it is. It's the day of celebrating Albert Hofmann, who was the first person to accidentally experience an acid trip back in 1943. It hit him while he was riding a bicycle and thus to this day, everyone calls it "Bicycle Day". This was my first bicycle day where I would trip to celebrate. The weather was beautiful, so I went down to Columbus Circle, 59th street right next to Central Park. I opened up a watermelon shaped card and saw two tabs sitting there.

"Enjoy your trip :)" is what was written inside the card.

Before you read the rest of this story, my advice is to not do drugs. If you need further details as to why, then just make sure you read until the end.

Both tabs landed on my tongue, and within the 45 minutes of sobriety I had left, I was able to rent a Citibike and started my big bicycle adventure within

Central Park. The LSD hit me as I was riding on the bike, and it felt incredible. The wind flew past my face, warm air with scents of flowers rushed into my nose, and I couldn't help but realize I wanted to record and document everything. Fun fact, riding a bike and filming is extremely difficult, let alone tripping at the same time. The thing about taking Lucy is that it's like a roller coaster. The build up to the peak of your trip can take some time, and so the beginning phase of this trip was tolerable. However, I remember when the hour and a half mark hit is when things started to get scary. I didn't have any water left at this point, and I was getting pretty thirsty. First, I returned my rented Citibike, then I went down to the subway on 59th street where they have places that sell food, drinks, etc. but all of the stores are underground. I remember heading towards the bathroom and saw the ceiling and the floor started to show multiple layers. It's like there were three floors moving sideways with multiple colors of that floor moving. The ceiling was doing the exact same thing. It was hard to walk straight while the echoes of the subways rippled in and out of my eardrums. When I realized the floors were moving I thought to myself,

"Uh oh. You really fucked up this time."

I headed to the bathroom and my friend, who I worked with at Starbucks at the time, came out of the restroom. She saw me and I soon explained my situation and how I was tripping major balls. She tried her best to calm me down and said I should go outside. She helped me get out of the subway system and make it above ground, to where I explained that I wanted to drink something. She pointed to a car that was selling smoothies. I walked up the car and explained I wanted a strawberry and banana smoothie with almond milk. As the man was making my smoothie, an older woman came right up to me and started talking about how she liked my hair. At this point in my life, I had blue dreadlocks that were tied up in the shape of a pineapple. It didn't help me while I was tripping because it would lead to random conversations with people, and when you are on an acid trip, talking to sober humans is very difficult. Sometimes it's very hard for your brain to come up with sentences that make sense.

This older woman explained she loved my hair and wanted to photograph me. I talked to her but avoided looking into her eyes as I was really high at this moment. I thought she'd take out her phone, but instead she whips out a giant fucking Canon camera with a ridiculous ass lens that seemed like it was in my whole face. Out of all the times people want to photograph me, it has to be the moment where everything I look at seems to have various shades of the color pallet appearing. At this point I got so uncomfortable, I ran back to my friend and explained I was too high to finish this smoothie transaction and that people were bothering me. I handed my friend the money and she soon brought back my smoothie. She explained that she had errands to run and suggested I drink my smoothie and go into nature in Central Park. I told her I was pretty scared but it seemed like the safest and closest choice for me to do.

Walking into Central Park, the bicycle carriage workers who were sitting on their bikes waiting for tourists to come by. They noticed me and all of them said hello. They asked me if I was feeling okay.

"I'm doing okay. I'm really high right now."

They laughed and said to enjoy my trip. With a little exhale of nervousness I breathed in and responded,

"Yeah, thanks. I'm trying."

I felt like a pinball bouncing around a machine inside Central Park. I remember it being super-hot, and after about two sips of my smoothie, I soon had anxiety that the place I got my drink from was sketchy. I thought it could've been poisoned so I put my smoothie in the trash. I also threw away my shoes. Yeah, my fucking shoes. I have proof. I ran into my ex-girlfriend in Central Park. I didn't know if she was real or just a hallucination because I was pretty high. She saw what I was going through and walked with me for a few minutes. Not gonna lie, I thought it was super hilarious that I was walking around Central Park without shoes on. I'm not a big fan of wearing them to begin with, but I figured I should wear shoes because my initial plan was to ride a bike, but since I was tripping so hard, I knew I wouldn't be hopping on another bike anytime soon. I asked my ex to snap a photo of me because I wanted to see what I looked like when I was sober later on. I just found it so fucking funny that I had no shoes on in New York. She explained that it's a city and that it's kinda gross that I'd perhaps have to be on the subway barefoot.

I told her that I wouldn't need shoes anymore because I'll move somewhere warm where I don't have to own any. I thought perhaps I'll buy sandals on my way home, but maybe once I was all sobered up.

The rest of the trip was extremely hard to remember. It was incredibly painful too. I remember going to a little fenced grass area with a tiny hill that had a blooming tree on top. It was somewhere on the west side of Central Park. The fence made it nice because I wouldn't be in the way of other people walking around. I had plenty of soft grass that was within this fenced in area where I was able to roam around like a child. I remember tripping so fucking hard that I realized why I was human. I explained to my ex that I understood the meaning of life and how incredible it is that trees grow, and humans can be alive all because of the sun. I thought at that moment that perhaps the sun was god. Sounds silly, right? It might be because my brain was lit up like a bonfire. LSD is the only drug that allows your brain to use 100% of itself at once. When you're sober, you only use about 15-20% of it at a time. Needless to say, I had some wild ass thoughts while high. I explained that I think I will die, but people will be obsessed with my death. They will find either my writing or my films, and they will realize I was onto something nobody else was thinking about. It only got recognition because I was dead. I always asked myself if god existed and to this day I don't know, but while tripping I realized that maybe he does exist because I believed that these events would happen when I died. This is what I tried explaining to my ex while I was tripping beyond any measure I have ever felt, but a lot of my words got tied up as I kept bouncing from topic to topic due to the number of ideas that were entering my mind. She started to film me, which was weird because I was trying to speak my thoughts. Again, another camera in my face. Even when I'm high, I can put together the pieces and see that someone is recording me. It gives me anxiety, even though I make videos all the time by myself, seeing somebody record me is weird, especially while I'm tripping. At this point I lost all control of my body. I was dehydrated, and I couldn't tell what was real and what wasn't real anymore. My vision was clouded with visuals of the tree, the sun, people, and my flower tattoo on my wrist that I would occasionally see. I didn't know what to do. I just kinda wandered around the grass field and started muttering words.

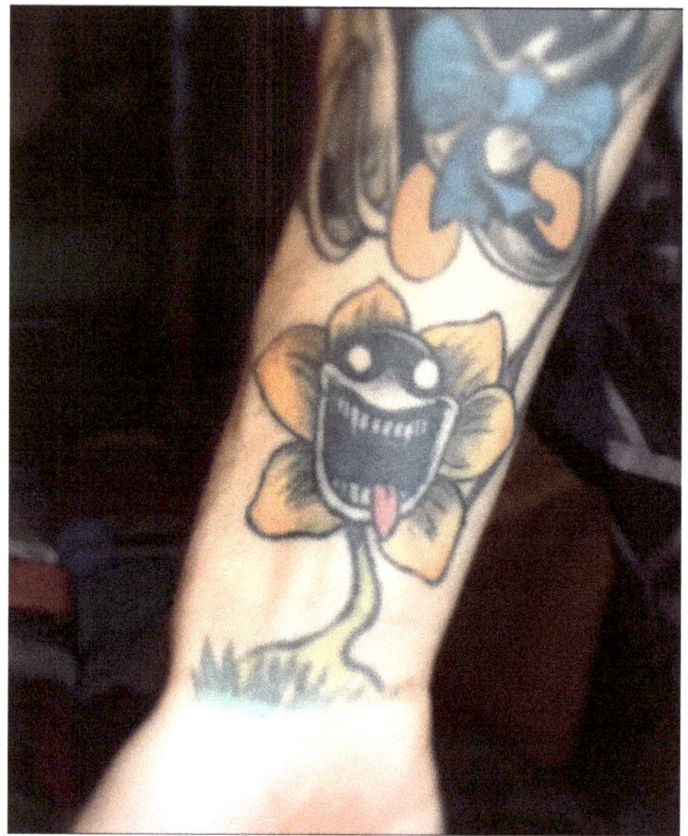

"One two one eight. One two one eight.
ONE TWO ONE EIGHT!"

My voice got loud. People started to stare. These numbers might not mean anything to you, but to me it was my lunch pin for school. We would have to type in our lunch code after we picked out what food we wanted, and it would bring up our school account where they would withdraw the money. Now you might ask yourself, "why was he screaming his lunch code?" It's my phone password. I was shouting out my phone password. It's not because I like that number, it's just something my brain would do when I wanted comfort. I would just look down at my phone, see my lock screen, punch in those numbers, and I could look at whatever I wanted or talk to whoever I wanted. However, I didn't have my phone, it was in my bag. I was too high to get it. I was just shouting my phone password as a signal for help because I was extremely uncomfortable. I've taken two tabs of LSD before but I had never felt like this. I felt my senses were overblown. I couldn't handle how many people there were, my ex recording me, and the fact that I was extremely dehydrated.

Black out. I don't remember what happened next. It's kinda like a snapshot of events. My vision would turn back on and I would realize what was happening for another two seconds and then blackout. I was in an incredible amount of pain. LSD had never done this to me and I don't know why this trip was different. My vision came back on, and the police were approaching me. Black out.

My eyeballs decide to turn back on and I realize that I'm screaming. It's not fun anymore. Make it stop. With my overblown senses and these random people touching me, it didn't make things better. It feels weird to have people holding me down. Are police officers holding me down? Another black out.

Again, my vision is restored, and I am in incredible amounts of pain. My legs are bound in a stretcher. I'm in what seems to be an ambulance truck. I scream. This man next to me tells me to shut up and holds his grip on my leg. I have a mini anxiety attack from this.

It doesn't surprise me though, it was a cop so I expect shitty treatment. However, I feel like I'm legit dying. The worst feeling in the entire world. Black out.

These black outs happen multiple times and every time I came to, there were random people around me. The last moment I remember was being in a building where lots of doctors surrounded me on a table and started grabbing at my arms. Again, I'm high as a kite so nothing is making sense anymore. Are these actual people? Are they harming me? Is that a needle? I scream endlessly. My breath is short but I am panicking. Black out. This time for a long time.

I'm woken up and I feel extremely tired. It's like I'm a walking zombie. The doctors explained that whatever I took that afternoon, it was laced with PCP. Instead of giving me one full dosage of sleepy stuff, they pumped two full dosages into my body because I wasn't falling asleep. I felt like a limp ragdoll as they had me stand up. To this day, this experience has traumatized me. I can't put into words what exactly I saw and felt during this trip. All I know is that I have to live with what things I saw and experienced. However, at the end of the day, I didn't have to walk home barefoot. After swiping my card in the hospital for $250 some dollars, I walked out of the building with socks on, so at least I wasn't barefoot on the subway home that night.

No Appearance From god

I grew up in a Christian household. At a young age, I was told Jesus was a person who died for my sins so that when I die, I don't have to burn in hell. It didn't really make any sense, but my parents wanted us to go to church, so we did. When I was a kid, I would imagine god sitting there in his/her cloud hearing my prayers, smiling down at me, moving their hands, and then casting down this magical sprinkle of power to make all my problems go away. We went to church less and less as we got older, but the belief in god's principles was still in place within my family household. Something different happened when I got older, I started to think for myself and not blindly trust or believe in things just because my pastor, grandparents, or parents told me to believe it. Over time, I kept seeing holes in this religion, and I'm gonna go ahead and state them all out.

First of all, I realize that there are lots of religions on this planet. However, I somehow ended up being born in USA, which a majority of the population follows the Christian belief system. If I say that I believe in Jesus and that he is my savior, then that means every other religion that exists out there, I claim they are all false and that mine is the real deal. Really? That's a bold statement to make. How do I not know Islam, Hinduism, Buddhism, or any other of the hundreds of religions that existed on this planet are the real deal? Not to mention there are thousands of historical religions that have died off because nobody is around to keep spreading the word of them. I grew up in a school system where our quizzes had multiple choice questions, and if you wanted to get the question right, you had to know what all the choices were before you made your decision to answer. Spoiler alert, I know almost nothing of what it means to be Muslim. I have no idea what your belief system is if you believe in Zoroastrianism. How am I supposed to really know for sure that Christianity is the one true religion if I don't know what the other religions are and what principles they consist of? I think it's a mistake to jump to conclusions and say Jesus is my savior and that every other religion is false just because I happened to be born in an area that is predominantly Christian based.

My second point is the silence I get from god. I realized that every time I prayed to god, sometimes I wouldn't hear anything back. That's a wack ass relationship. If you are friends with someone and you do all the talking with keeping the relationship and the other person just leaves your ass on read, it's not fun. What the hell kind of relationship is that? In the bible it claims people saw Jesus cure blind people, rise from the dead, hell even Moses claims god spoke directly to him. If these events happened to me, then maybe I would start believing in god. Other people who were alive then got to witness this, so why hasn't there been any appearance since then? Did people just take mushrooms, see hallucinations, and to them those visuals were god? Maybe Mary had an affair with another man, and in order to get out of being accused of cheating on Joseph, she made up an elaborate story that the chosen one of god is in her stomach. We have no idea if any of these outcomes are true, all I know is that if god has all the power entirely, it shouldn't be that hard to send an angel messenger down and tell me the truth directly to my face. I can't just blindly rely on faith to know he exists.

Third point is that this book was written a very long time ago. In fact, it states in the bible that women were giving birth to kids at age 10 or 11, because that's when their bodies were able to reproduce. It claims in the bible that you have to wait for marriage until you have sex, but for 2021, we live within society, which means you have to turn 18 to get married. If you are really smart, you'll wait till after college, so that means 23 or 24. It might take some time to meet somebody and date them until they accept your proposal so probably late 20's or early 30's. Are you kidding me? We all have sexual urges when we are teenagers. How the fuck am I supposed to wait until then to have sex? And masturbating is a sin, so you can't relieve yourself that way either. It's purely unwinnable. I'm not saying kids should be allowed to have sex, I grew up within a society and the rules of waiting to 18 makes sense, however simply telling people they can't have an orgasm until they are married is kinda ridiculous. I know as a boy, if you wait super long to the point where you have sexual build up, it's hard to focus on the most mundane tasks. You'll just be watching a movie and all of the sudden you see a female appear, and your mind goes bananas. I think saying masturbating or having sex before 18 makes having these sexual urges hard to deal with. Just teach people about condoms and ways to prevent pregnancy instead of forcing your children to just not think about sex, because in most cases, it's almost impossible to just ignore any sexual urges you have in your mind.

Last point is that Christianity is almost like a "build a bear workshop" environment. If you don't know what that is, it's a store where you go and pick out a bear, stuff it, and choose which outfit it will wear. It's simply a pick and build your own stuffed animal store for kids. They get to choose what their bear gets to look like, so there are no rules when it comes to what they want. If you want to go in and not put any clothes on your bear, there is nothing stopping you from walking out with a naked bear. Mainstream Christianity has kind of the same presence of picking and choosing things to believe in. The bible is written clear as day, but people seem to no longer follow parts of them anymore. It's like they read some sections and seem to follow every word but then choose to not even consider other parts of their holy book. So... you're just creating your own religion with inspirations from Christianity? Doesn't make any sense to me. Why even call yourself a Christian at that point? If I believe in something, I'm gonna follow it to every core principle that it has. It baffles me that some people ignore certain aspects of what is written in the bible but other rules that are in there, they blow out of proportion and think that it's an extremely big deal to follow them. Make up your mind. If you believe in something, I expect you to be eating the whole cake and not just a couple of slices of your choosing. Perhaps you don't like the whole cake, fine by me. I advise you should relabel yourself because you aren't actually in that particular religion, you've simply made your own.

Let's say tomorrow god decides to come down from heaven, make his grand entrance into my life, tells me that he exists, he explains that I should stop doubting and believe in him. No questions asked, I would have enough evidence to believe in god, but that doesn't mean I would like him. In fact, if god does exist, I'd like him to know I'm kinda upset at him. What is his grand master plan he has for creating people and sending us down here into this simulation? There are so many people that get created and are raised or stuck in areas on this planet that give them miserable experiences. War, violence, greed, and other horrific things happen to people. Some humans die from missiles being shot at them, or get raped and have to live with traumatic experiences, yet god doesn't step in. You might argue that all these incidents are done by other humans, thus the root of the problem is sin that is causing these issues. Fair argument, but what about those people who die from natural disasters such as tornadoes or floods? If anybody is in control of that shit, it's god so why does he choose to allow that to happen?

They say god is almighty and powerful, and that he has the ability to do anything, so we should fear him, otherwise we will be sent to hell. If god happens to have all the power in the entire universe, he knows exactly what you will do in your whole lifetime even before creating you. How the fuck can you create somebody and say you love them up and down when you know ahead of time that when they die, they have a straight ticket to hell because they don't believe in you as their god. I am completely clueless with this fucking question and not a single soul on this planet has an answer to it. Hey god, if you exist, this "believe in me or you go burn in hell forever" is a stupid scare tactic to make people believe in you. It's a shitty thumbnail a lot of people "click on" because they are horrified at the thought of dying forever, and if that's what you need to do to get the attention of humans to stroke your ego, I am more embarrassed and sorry for you.

Listen, if you need to believe in something to be a better person, fine by me. In fact, I'm thankful I was Christian because I've walked away from the religion with some principles I still follow. Just don't be an asshole when it comes to your religion. Accept the fact that not everyone is going to join your cult and be a part of your team, but don't treat them any differently either. I think somewhere in that ancient book it says you're supposed to love your neighbor like you love yourself, but I guess some people stopped following that bible verse too.

My guess as to why people blindly believe in a religion is due to the fact that they are spoon fed fear as soon as they are born. I think a lot of people are scared shitless of death. We don't really know scientifically what happens when you die other than your heart stops beating. Lots of people need something else to relieve their minds from overthinking this outcome that we all will experience one day in our lives. Perhaps nothing actually happens. Imagine you don't go to heaven when your life slips between your fingers. What if there is no reincarnation? Perhaps death is simply a black screen of nothing. My brain can't even imagine what nothing is, but that could be an outcome to what happens when we die. Can it be that we are just extremely lucky to be alive and other than this one life, this is all we have? I can't tell you. I'll probably never know the answer, and neither will you. I don't think the thought of nothing happening after you die should dwindle or hurt the time you have on this planet, but it could be an outcome. I just have trouble picturing what nothing is. It's not darkness because darkness itself is something, and it's not sleep or blindness either because those are things too. I don't actually have the slightest clue of what death is.

Maybe you believe in god because you've had a personal experience with him. Don't let my opinion knock your faith over. I hope god gives you every thing you ever wanted in your life and more. As of right now for me, there has been no appearance from god. I can't imagine it'll happen anytime soon, but if god does appear I'll be angry at that dude. Why did you create earth with so many horrible things that happen to people? How come you showed yourself to others back in the day but not to me? Why do we have to follow rules in a book that don't make sense with today's society? What plausible answer do you have to explain letting other humans hurt and terrify each other? You expect people to believe in you and worship you as you let these things happen on this planet? This is a fucking sick ass game you're allowing to play out. Hope you're enjoying yourself. Amen.

Growing Up Is Phony

If I could be best friends with somebody who never existed, it easily would be Holden Caulfield. He's a fictional character written in the book *The Catcher in the Rye*. The book is about a depressed teenager who is struggling with getting older. I was assigned to read this book for high school, which happens to be a time period where we are being taught to hopefully be sent off to college, to which we will train ourselves to acquire skills, and in the end we'll land an entry level job where we'll be able to buy a house, pay our bills, and maybe have a few kids along the way. Sounds like a life that society assumes we all want to live. It's the truth though, that's why the whole public education system, at least in America, is pretty screwed up, but if it wasn't for the fucked up school system, I wouldn't have met my imaginary friend, Holden Caulfield.

What typically happens when you cross paths with old friends or acquaintances out of the blue? Most of the time they will ask how you are doing, and will discuss with you what is going on in their life. Holden despises these conversations whenever he runs into old friends in the city. He calls them phony because he dislikes how people talk about their life and how great it is, despite him being able to see signs that maybe they are actually unhappy. I think in a lot of ways we as humans want to show everyone that our lives are fantastic, amazing, or whatever dumb synonym you wanna use. Let's just be real with each other, sometimes being a human on this planet sucks ass. Think about it, to make it through life comfortably, you have to have money, power, status, and all that other bullshit. I don't wanna kiss ass to some company for years in hopes they will give me a promotion so I can pay my loans on a house in the suburbs. Fuck that. I understand why Holden throws the word phony at people who talk about how grand their life is. Just be honest with how your life is going to others. Maybe some things are good and that's great. I'm happy for you, but is everything truly what you wanted? Are all your expectations of life meeting your fulfillment? Probably not, but on the off-chance that all your dreams do come true, try not to rub it in everyone else's faces. More than likely, other people are barely able to pay their bills, so be humble for your comfortability, and hopefully give some good advice to those who aren't as lucky as you.

There is one thing that is phonier than people talking about their phenomenal lives, and that's getting older. Nothing like a step closer to my human body aging to a point where it's vulnerable to giving up on pumping blood, nice. Seems like Holden shares the same viewpoint. He understands the world is pretty intense. It revolves around money, and people often don't give a damn about what is happening to you. Things break down or stop working when they get to a certain age. Cars, sweaters, computers, shoes, you name it. The worst is when people get older. Ever have a relative or friend that you get to watch grow up? Their child-like imagination of thinking anything is possible gets squashed into oblivion as they enter the world and understand the terms of service of what it means to be a human within society.

It is truly sad to spectate others getting older. Holden struggles with this due to his little sister Phoebe attending elementary school and she ends up going on the same field trips he went on when he was a little kid. One of the places they went to is the Natural History Museum in New York City. I'm not sure if you have ever been there, but they have all sorts of cool things to look at. From space, to animals, even old environmental changes on earth, it has a little bit of everything of what we know our planet has been through. Holden talks about how his little sister will go on this field trip and will see the Native Americans statues behind this wall of glass. She'll be able to witness a brief capture of what these people did to survive living in North America. The same scene he saw when he was a child will still be the exact thing she sees. Nothing will have changed. It's like a moment frozen in time. The only thing that actually has changed is the people who have entered the museum and observed this scene. Holden wishes that he himself could freeze moments in time, just like the Native Americans that are locked in time within the museum. Imagine being able to take people or places and have them stay exactly the way they are. It would be nice. There's a lot of things that I wouldn't like to age, just for the sake of my comfortability of not having to go through the difficult emotions of dealing with fixing old objects that break down, or having to say goodbye to loved ones who pass on. Sadly, there is no pause button to things we want to have halted in life, we just have to learn to deal with it.

When I was working in GameStop at 18 years old, I watched a little kid come in and start looking for a video game. I asked his dad if they had any questions and they asked if we had the video game *Animal Crossing.* This game is about moving to a random island where all your neighbors are animals, and you are the only human. You have a house and get to do fun things like fishing, catching bugs, growing trees, and selling things such as fossils or furniture items for money. You can use your money to pay off your loan, which expands your house, or spend it on different cosmetics for your character or home. I checked behind the counter and found a copy of *Animal Crossing.* I remember the kid being super ecstatic that we had a copy and he jumped up and down with a smile due to his overwhelming amount of excitement. This whole scene reminded me of going to GameStop years ago where the same scene unfolded when my father bought me an older version of *Animal Crossing.* The exact thing happened here, only it was a new boy who couldn't wait to play the same game I played, and will probably have the same experiences of making friends with villagers and decorating his island. The funny thing about this is that *Animal Crossing* is a game about doing things you would do as a grownup such as paying your mortgage, yet when it comes to a video game where you can do all of this with bright colors and fancy rewards, it's fun. I realized that simply because I grew up and that memory of me being excited was gone, the memory relived itself as I sold this kid his copy of *Animal Crossing.* It was bittersweet due to the fact I knew one day this child may look back at this fond memory and miss it just like I do. Hope you pay your bills in game on time kid, it's good practice for when you get older.

There is one thing I dislike about *The Catcher in the Rye* and it's the fact that the book kinda ends abruptly. I remember rushing into the living room and both my parents were watching TV. I explained to them a quick summary of the book, and how the last chapter just basically has Holden explain how he is in a mental ward and doesn't want to talk anymore. I was frustrated. I got so emotionally attached to this character and he just reels in my attention for 277 pages and it just ends because he doesn't wanna share anything else. I felt like the author, J. D. Salinger, was just sick of writing this phony book and decided to be done with it. How can you do this? My parents remember me raging about the book as they sat in the living room with their movie on pause, nodding their heads until my rant was over with.

Now that I'm older, I've digested this ending and come to terms that it relates to growing up. Sometimes when we get older, it just kinda happens abruptly. One day you're allowed to go to school and play with toys for a majority of the day, and then boom, you gotta start doing homework assignments and handing them in on time. Don't get too used to this, because eventually you're gonna have to clock in and start slaving at a minimum wage job to afford your college textbooks. Not so fast, you thought you were off the hook? Time to do something big in your life so you feel like you have the importance of staying alive. Life just keeps going and doesn't stop. The gray hairs will come in, the wrinkles will start to appear, and your last breath will hit your lungs. Now that I write about growing up for this long, I realize why Holden throws phony everywhere in his life. It does suck. Not all of life, but the fact that one day the fun days grow to an end is sad to think about. Makes me believe that growing up is phony, regardless of the wisdom and memories that come with it. Too bad I can't apply to a career where I can be a catcher within a rye field. I think I'd do a good job of saving people from jumping off a cliff to their impending doom of getting older.

Life is a weird video game where a bunch of things hit you, and it may dwindle your life points down to zero. However, even once the game of life ends, a lot of the levels were fun and exciting. Maybe it's worth playing the game all the way through, even though my character might not be as nimble or bright eyed as he was in the beginning. Regardless of knowing that the game will end, the adventure as a whole will have levels where I will mostly find things I enjoy, even if the level ends up being an annoying water level, then perhaps I'll only enjoy the music or something. If I get to pick some party members to be in my squad, Holden will always have a place. He might find the whole game dumb, stupid, or phony, but I'll explain he should press the ready up button to play anyways because some levels in my life have been worth it, so the future might hold some great experiences too.

GAME PAUSED

My parents once told me that if they could've done anything differently with raising me, they wouldn't have put a video game controller in my hands at the age of four. To this day, I still play games almost every day. It's my favorite type of escapism from reality. Perhaps it's the heart pounding gameplay, or maybe I get intrigued by the story, either or, you'll find that I've dabbled in just about every video game.

The very first video game I played was *Crash Bandicoot* on the PlayStation. Sad thing for me is that at the time, we had no memory card for our console. It didn't matter what level I got to that day or however long I decided to play for, I would be forced to replay the same levels over and over again if I ever shut off the PlayStation in our living room. Call me old school, but this is the pain and suffering I had to go through when I was a child. Eventually we got a memory card and I was able to finally save my progress and start beating games in the library. *Crash Bandicoot Warped, Tekken 3, Croc: Legend of the Gobbos, Twisted Metal, Crash Bash*, and many more titles.

In first grade, I met a kid in school who told me about Mario. This Italian plumber was a brand-new character to me at the age seven and soon I found a GameCube that I unwrapped from a Christmas present. Games like *Super Mario Sunshine, Golden Eye*, various Sonic games, *Super Smash Bros*, and *Mario Kart* were played within my bedroom. I remember playing my GameCube for so long, that one day it stopped working. I legit burnt my little purple cube console out to exhaustion. I was devastated. Didn't know what to do with my free time. For a while I was unable to play any games, and my parents could tell it bummed me out. One day, as I hopped in my mom's car as she picked me up after school, she asked me to move the groceries over to the backseat. She must have just went shopping and gotten some things before coming to my school. I moved some bags over and saw a GameCube box underneath all of those grocery bags. Needless to say, I was beyond stoked to be able to continue my journeys on the television.

I'd make friends in school through the topic of video games. It was a common thing I got to talk about with other people in my class, simply because if they didn't play one game, there was usually another game they played that they would talk to me about. It's how I was able to learn about new titles people liked. Eventually, I was told I should play an online game called *Runescape*. Rumor had it, this game was an online game where I could meet up with my friends and play together, which for 2007, was a crazy experience to have within your home. I remember coming home and installing *Runescape* onto the PC in the living room. The computer used to be my older brother's computer that was upstairs in his room, but after discussing with my parents that I had an interest in playing computer games with my friends, they decided to move my brother's computer into the living room so they could keep an eye on me as I played. In all honesty, I ought to thank my older brother for taking one for the team. If he wasn't willing to move his PC downstairs for me to use, I wouldn't have a way to play any computer games.

I created my character and named him runematt18, and away I went. This game is a fantasy game, where you can train various skills like attack, archery, magic, and other common skills like cooking, woodcutting, fishing, etc. The game has so much to do that it was popular in my school for several years. However, it didn't take long for my parents to come around and realize I was playing a game with magic in it, and soon they told me I was unable to play this game. My parents were a bit overprotective when it came to their children, especially in ways of us learning about magic or mythical creatures. I have no idea what my mom or dad watched or read in the 90s, but I wasn't allowed to watch *Harry Potter*, play *Pokémon*, or even try to install and have fun in games that had wizards in it. As a child I was so confused, but I guess it refers to my parents being Christian and them reading or learning something online that stated their kids could be tempted away from the religion if they were involved in these activities. I had a couple of weeks in *Runescape* that were good times. Adventuring around with my friends in the game, suddenly realizing one of my friends disconnected because their parents made a call on their landline phone so they lost internet, passing by an area another friend was at and only seeing their bronze helmet and a pile of bones laying on the ground, to which I came to the conclusion they got murdered by the nearby skeleton monsters, all sorts of fond memories. However, once my parents passed by the computer one day and saw me casting fire spells, it was game over for my time in *Runescape*.

My very first all-nighter I pulled in my life was because of a video game. I had moved to California near the end of my 8th grade year, and I was away from friends I had grown up with, however one of these friends and I still played online PC games to catch up and have a good time. He told me of a brand new open world online game titled *Guild Wars 2* would be released in August 2012. The game would launch a month before school started which was a perfect time to stay up and game with my friend. We awaited several months for this game to release, and once it did, I told my mother I would be playing the game late. I rolled a character as a thief profession, which to those who don't play online games, a thief is a character class who is sneaky and uses elements of hiding to pop out and attack enemies with swords and pistols, so I wasn't using any magic in the game, meaning my parents would have no reason to kick me off playing this one. My mom came into my room around 10pm at night and told me she was heading to sleep. I said goodnight to her and immediately put my eyes back onto my PC monitor. Around 7:30am in the morning, my mother walks into my room and finds me in the same spot I was at the night before.

"Did you stay up all night?" She asked me with a surprised tone.

I simply shake my head, with noticeable bags under my eyes. I logged off the game and headed to bed. What a way to lose my "pulling an all-nighter virginity" with a video game. It perfectly fits me as a person that a game would give me the decision to stay up so late and choose to be tired to simply have a taste of adventure and roam around in a brand new world with my friend. I don't regret it, and to this day I occasionally play *Guild Wars 2*.

When it comes to which game I play, I know exactly what I like and dislike. As people on this planet, we often know what kind of adventures we want to go on and this is why we launch ourselves into these virtual worlds. However, there comes a time, even when the game is full of eye catching moments, we hit the pause button. The game world stops, and the reality of life hits you back in the face. Maybe you pause because you have to use the bathroom. Perhaps you hit that button because you have to check your laundry. That doesn't mean you'll never play the game again. Most of the time, we want to try to accomplish a task before giving up. Hence, more often than not, you'll see me press that button in the middle of my control and the game will keep showing me its vibrant colors.

What if I told you that our human experience on this planet has pauses too? You might think that's weird, because the sun keeps moving, and the cars will never stop driving on the roads, but if you look closely, you might find that life does have its beats where we take a moment and focus on something else. Maybe we hit the pause button in life because another person enters our world. If we ever pause our journey, it doesn't mean we've given up on our adventure, it simply means our attention has to be shifted and given elsewhere. Our drive for projects or jobs does diminish. The taste in our mouths changes and we crave other foods. Each eyeball in our heads seems to get bored of the same environments and they desperately call out for new sights to see. Every vibration of noise that ripples in our ears can grow repetitive, and there may come a time you start listening to other beeps and boops that burst out of your headphones.

What I'm trying to say is, sometimes you may think you have your life figured out, and you assume you know exactly what game you want to play, but there will be sudden moments where you realize maybe you don't know what you want. Perhaps the game you've been playing isn't as exciting as it used to be. After all, there are loads of games to play. From racing, shooter, platformer, puzzle, fighting, you name it. How on earth can you know the game you're currently playing is the one you'll finish when you have so many other titles to try? That's why in life, you'll often find yourself taking a break on various different things you have going on. Our society may tell you at a young age that you have to eat all the food on your plate, but I'm here to say, it's okay to step away. Here's a cheat code for you. You're allowed to put your game of life on pause.

Just because we press the button that freezes our game and the words "GAME PAUSED" appears on the screen, it doesn't mean we will never return to see the ending of that adventure. Maybe one day you'll pick that paintbrush back up and complete that picture. Who knows if you'll get that degree in that subject you studied for years. Only you get to decide what the next level in your life is going to be. Nobody is forcing you to play a bad game. Regardless of how long you press the buttons on your controller, every game, and human life, has it's time where it comes to an end. No glitches or memory cards will help you backtrack the clock, so you might as well play a game, with game-play, music and graphics that you enjoy 100%.

Don't Be Sorry, Just Don't Do It

I remember it was a harsh reality to realize earth spins in peace because we trade coins or pieces of paper to each other in return of food or services. It was also a hard pill to swallow the fact that most of my life will be spent doing things I don't want to do so that I can acquire this kind of currency. It's a bummer to realize that being an adult isn't quite as fun with all the responsibilities you have on your plate to keep yourself alive. The only reason I am in this flesh body and have to chase money to live is because my parents fucked one day back in 1995.

My parents aren't bad people, in fact I'm thankful to have them in my life. Let me set the stage, my dad met my mother while they were in college, they dated for 6 months and ran off to get married, heck even my grandparents didn't meet my mother until after they put a ring on it. Believe it or not, they are still together to this day. Not sure why my mother married my dad, he tried to impress her one day by jumping his lifted pickup truck over quicksand, but his truck got stuck and he had to carry my mom out of the sinking vehicle to safety. I have three siblings, two older brothers and one younger. My mother was a stay-at-home mom and took care of us while maintaining the house. My father worked as a headhunter, and if you are thinking a headhunter means he is some bounty hunter who tracks people down, you're wrong. A headhunter is somebody who finds people to fill positions within a company. Sounds like a boring job to me, but it paid the bills so my dad did it.

The first time I realized humans can have money problems is when my dad lost his job during the recession in 2010. We ended up having to move out of our home in Michigan because my father was unable to pay the loans he had on the house. One day we hopped in a moving van and drove to California, which is where my dad was able to find a new job. It was bizarre to pack your bags and move away from family relatives and friends I grew up with. Took me awhile to fit into a new school environment and get used to not having snow on the ground during Christmas. I was also a teenager, meaning I was facing my own problems of growing up while moving, it was a weird combination to juggle.

Anywho, I struggled a lot to talk to people, like in front of the class during presentations. I embarrassed myself by having a mini anxiety attack one day while having to present a stupid "science in the news" presentation. My knees shook, my voice was weak, and I just stopped talking for ten whole seconds. I put my news article down and simply stared at all the eyes looking at me. I gave a pretty mean glance to my science teacher who was the mastermind to making us all present our papers in front of the class. He shook a tin can full of wooden sticks and pulled out one with our names on it. If your name was spoken out, that would mean you would have to walk to the front of the class and present your work. The sticks hitting the tin can was a horrible sound to hear. I swear, he shook that can around for so long, it made my anxiety of presenting just grow in anticipation of having to step in front of everyone. This meltdown in class made me realize I had to face my fear and try to defeat my anxiety to be able to talk comfortably in front of large groups of people.

To overcome my fear, I threw myself into theatre and improv classes. One time I stumbled into a room where they were having improv tryouts and I realized there were about forty or fifty kids inside this classroom. I got scared and decided I was gonna leave instead. Before I could walk out the door, two other students walked up to me and asked me why I was leaving. They talked me into staying, saying that it could be fun if I auditioned for the team. Luckily, I was able to get more comfortable with talking to others by paying attention and making friends in my theatre classes. I even had the courage to audition for plays and musicals. Not gonna lie, I was pretty surprised to see my name on the cast list for these productions. A wave of confidence hit me, and I thought I found my place in life. Figured I could try to become an actor because it was one of the only things I looked forward to doing other than playing video games. My dad always said video games could never be a career, and it seemed like a lot of people would go watch improv shows, plays, and musicals I was in, so to me it seemed like the best career choice.

I remember telling my father I wanted to become a theatre major and he straight up said no, advising me that I would make no money when it came to performing on stage. He did a good job at painting the picture to how difficult it would be to make it in the world of film or theatre. I'd have to go to audition after audition, get told no multiple times, and just because I was able to get cast in productions in high school didn't mean I had any talent. Little depressing to hear because theatre and improv were the only things I ended up spending time on during after school hours. Made me feel a little lost because I didn't know what to major in for college. My dad said to go into the computer science field or business. After some time thinking, I thought since I liked video games I could try and become a programmer and major in computer science.

Little did I know, studying computer science didn't mean you would make video games. It meant you would learn code so that you could potentially become a programmer for businesses who need websites, software to run on their machines, and other pointless boring shit that made me want to sleep during my classes. No video game building courses, no modeling or rigging of characters within animation software, nothing. I felt lost. My drive for school, which was doing shows after class, wasn't there in college and it made me incredibly depressed. I told my parents I was thinking of auditioning for shows in college and yet again, my dad said no. He told me to focus on my classes and that theatre shows would just distract me from my work. You think I listened to his advice? Hell no.

I remember going to audition for a show, and all these theatre majors were there and saw me as an outsider. It was strange because a lot of them were jealous that I ended up getting a big role in a production since most of them were studying to become actors and found me as competition. Not gonna lie, it felt really good appearing out of fucking nowhere and just acing the audition. Made me feel like I was a secret character you unlocked for *Super Smash bros.* Anywho, I knew if I told my dad he would be pissed, so I decided to wait until I had a family dinner where my brothers, their girlfriends and other family relatives were there. It was at that moment I told everyone that I made it into a theatre production at my college. Everyone in the room was super proud of me and told me they were excited, everyone except my dad who was flat out angry, but he didn't want to say anything, so he just gave me this weird ass look. I could only tell because his eyes stared directly into my fucking soul at the dinner table upon announcing my recent success. It was hilarious to me because we had to continue the evening eating dinner until everyone went home. Then he could start fuming at me.

Took some time to make him realize that I wasn't going to change my mind. He threatened to stop paying for my education if my grades ended up slipping because of my involvement within theatre at my university. Education in America is horribly expensive, to the point where they just milk the shit out of every 18-year-old who graduates from high school. They brainwash everyone in school to get an education so that you can get a job, but in reality, colleges in America are just a business. They end up building more buildings and hiring more people because kids have to take out loans for 30,000 - 200,000 for education depending on the university they attend. Believe it or not, it's almost impossible to take out a loan when it comes to affording a mortgage for a house in your early twenties, however if you need to go to school, the bank has no problem whipping out loads of student loans for you to carry around for the remaining duration of your life. Fuck capitalism. Anywho, I had to rely on my dad for college, so I made sure my grades didn't slip,

I ended up performing in this production and I felt that I grew so much as an actor due to having theatre professors who gave me advice and pointers on my acting. I ended up secretly taking theatre classes because I had intentions of at least minoring in theatre. Soon I realized that I started to fit in more with the people in my theatre classes then my computer science courses. I'll be honest, I couldn't see myself staring at a screen all day and being around other people who were socially awkward and didn't know how to talk to each other. I felt more comfortable around those studying theatre, since they were able to look you in your eyes and have a conversation. Those people felt more real, compared to the A.I. social skills my fellow computer loving student majors had. After the show ended, my whole brain switched into trying to study theatre. I remember sitting my parents down and explained to them that I didn't want to learn code anymore, I wanted to act. My father straight up said absolutely not and told me that I would never find work. The explanation he gave was to make sure I was setup to study something that would land me a job to get me enough money in the future. He mentioned that if I wanted to switch majors, I would have to pay for it directly out of my pocket and he wouldn't help me whatsoever. To be honest, I felt like I disappointed my father because I was set on trying to study something that he had no confidence in, I didn't want to graduate in a subject I had no passion for. At the end of the day, I felt like I failed my father's expectations.

I told him sorry and that I hoped he would understand how I felt.

"Don't be sorry, just don't do it."

This was always my dad's response to random shit we did that made him upset. If we ever hurt one of our brothers, woke up late for work or made a mess in the kitchen and didn't clean up, he would say this as a response. We'd always realized that we made a mistake so we would apologize, which is something you should do. I think being sorry is an important thing to feel and voice out, but it seemed my dad didn't like this word, and this would always be his direct response in return if he heard one of us apologize. When he said it this time in regards to me wanting to do something else with my life, I felt really annoyed. It was the first time I didn't listen to his advice and would end up trying to become an actor. I realized that I'd rather have little money, but as long as I was doing something I enjoyed, it would lead to a happier life. The last thing I wanted to do is get stuck doing a job I didn't like for the rest of my life

I couldn't attend my college anymore because my dad stopped paying for me, so I was in a pickle. My choices were either to audition for things in Michigan, which to be honest there's almost no theatre opportunity for people to grow in the mitten shaped land, or try to figure out a way to audition in another place with more options. This state is known for producing cars and its nature, that's about it. I didn't know what to do. Luckily, I was dating a girl at the time who applied to NYU and got accepted. She wanted to move to New York City to study film, which is a perfect city to attempt to become an actor, way better than Michigan. My decision was made, I told my parents I was moving to New York. I sold a lot of my belongings and left June 30th, 2017, for the big apple. It was kinda weird because it would be the first time I started a journey without my parents, brothers, or friends nearby. This decision would affect my future in ways I would never know. I thought on the horizon I would see city adventures, theatre roles, and working. Little did I know that in my future there would be city adventures, a drug addiction, and lots of fucking working.

You're Not The First Person

Being in love can make you blind, so much so that you might as well have put a blindfold over my eyes because I could hardly see the blatantly obvious red flags in my past relationship. I was living with my girlfriend at the time in Flint, Michigan. It was close to our university and rent was dirt cheap due to the water crisis. She had never moved out of Michigan, so when it came to living in New York City, she struggled because it took time for her to make friends in school and an overwhelming amount of stress due to us having to pay city rent. I already moved from Michigan to California and went through this process of feeling alone and realized that it would take time to find my place in a new environment. I think because I went through this already, it didn't affect me as much as it did for her. Regardless, she was important to me, so I made sure to try and make life easier for her.

Before we jump into this tale, this chapter might sound like my ex was such a horrible person, but the truth is that I had a lot of good memories with her, and I appreciate everything I learned from that relationship, however it ended very badly. I'll share this story since it affected me well into the future. We moved into our apartment in Astoria at the beginning of July 2017. We lived in Queens because rent was cheaper there, and it was only a 20-25 minute subway ride to get into the city. Once we moved in, she hung a poster above our bed from the band *Joy Division* that had written "Love will tear us apart".

Nothing wrong with the band *Joy Division*, but it's kind of weird to have this quote above your bed, especially when you know what the song lyrics are saying. We already had a weird part in our relationship before we moved where her ex-boyfriend kissed her. She told me about the event on the same day when it happened. She felt horrible about the incident and insisted on breaking up, but I told her that it was nice she talked to me about it as soon as possible and we ended up working things out. If I was smart, I would've known that was a red flag warning, but to me I was blind as a bat. I still hopped in the moving van with her and moved to New York City on that hot summer day.

After she started her semester at NYU, she was busy with school and trying to work in order to pay her half of rent. I ended up getting into NYIT for Film, but I was unable to attend due to not being able to take out loans. With no cosigner, the bank wasn't willing to hand me student loans. At the time I was pretty upset about it, but I'm quite happy to not have any loans now. Since I wasn't going to college, I was working several jobs. One was at Starbucks at 59th St Station, another small job at a restaurant called Landmarc in the Time Warner building, a seasonal job teaching computer skills at Lehman College to kids, and I started another gig in the fall at a place called Blue Balloons where we dressed up as superheroes or other various characters and attended different birthday parties for children. Even with the handful of jobs, money was tough, and if I was working a lot and somehow had extra money, I typically took it easy and stayed home to save money, unless friends from out of state came to visit, then I would make an excuse to explore the city.

Regardless, I made sure to put as much free time I had when I wasn't working into my relationship. I could tell the city life was hard for my girlfriend. It didn't help that she went to a private school where the tuition was super expensive, so most of the students there had mommy and daddy paying for their school and rent, while she was taking out loans and working in order to afford living in the city. Oftentimes she'd come home as beat as I was, and would typically share her frustration of having trouble fitting in. I told her that the right people would come along after some time. New York City has tons of humans, and eventually they would enter her life. I should've watched my words, because more entered my girlfriend then I would have liked.

I remember when it started getting colder, our relationship was hitting a rocky path. More time was spent on her phone, and she wanted less time with me. It hurt me because we shared a room together, so it's not like I had a choice of going somewhere else if she didn't want to see me, but we just had to deal with it. I tried to make sure she knew that if she ever wanted to talk to me she was more than welcome to, but she just voiced her stress with school and mentioned she didn't want to be bothered.

One day she told me that she wanted to spend the night with some new girls she had met at her university. I was happy that she was finding new friends and told her it was a great idea. I told her while she was sleeping over her friend's place, I would go see a band live that night called *The Shacks*. On my way to the concert, I ran into my girlfriend on the street, she was on her way to her friend's place with her overnight bag. We talked and I told her I was heading to the concert and wished for her to have fun with her friends. She told me goodbye, but she said bye as if I was her friend, just saying bye and walking past me. No hug, no kiss, nothing that made it seem like I was even dating this person. It made me feel so strange. Do you ever have those moments where you know something is wrong, but you can't put your finger on it? That's exactly how I felt.

I remember going to this concert and getting a little drunk. Felt so weird to be in a place with so many people and yet nobody was willing to talk to me. Can't say I blame them, everyone came to hear the music. I remember hearing *The Shacks* play and having one too many ciders. I took an Uber home and felt so sick to my stomach. I couldn't wait to get out of that horrible car because the momentum of each left and right turn from the back of the vehicle made me feel like absolute trash. The minute my driver got to my apartment, I opened the door and threw up on the street. What a shit night.

Fast forward a day later, and my girlfriend received an early Christmas gift of a paid flight back to our home state of Michigan, that way she could see her family a little bit for the holidays. It was just her going though, I would be staying in New York and keep working. I didn't have the extra money to pay for a ticket to go with her. She woke up in the morning to shower, and I had to wake up and get ready to be a wage slave at Starbucks. I remember seeing her phone unplugged and realized that she may want it charged for her flight to Michigan. I grabbed her phone and plugged it in, her home screen blinked on and the big battery symbol with 43% appeared on the screen. It disappeared a second later and the first message on her front page was the following:

"The sex was great. :)"

That shit hit me like a bullet in the chest. I was overwhelmed with emotion. Did she really just go sleep with someone and then have the decency to hop back in bed this weekend and sleep next to me? It's a complete recipe for a psychopath. Now let me remind you, I didn't even unlock her phone, all I did was plug it in for her so that she could have a charged phone, and this message appeared on her home screen, so I was able to find out about this just by chance. I'm thankful my good intention ended up stumbling upon this message, because at this moment, it was my business now. I ended up opening her phone and looked at her messages with this dude, and sure enough there was enough proof that they had slept together. They had text messages of flirting and planning to meetup the day she said she was having a "girl's night". Inside her photo gallery she even had a photo of him at a diner the next morning. I was livid. To this day, my ex never found out about how I realized she cheated on me, so if you are reading this right now, maybe next time you sleep with somebody while you are already dating and living with another guy, I suggest putting a password on your phone before doing so. I started pacing back and forth in the room. Do I talk to her about it now? I'm so emotional so maybe I should wait. I was furious. I was also late for work. She came out of the bathroom and she saw I was upset. She then had the guts to say the following,

"Matthew, don't be jealous that I am going to Michigan and you're not. You need to stop acting like a child."

I looked at her dead in the eye and told her that she had no idea how I was feeling at that moment. I looked at the clock, realized I was late for work, told her I had to leave, and I left the room.

I bursted into the backdoor of the Starbucks I worked at and all my co-workers knew something was up. I told them what was on my plate and they all felt horrible for me. It was the first time I was given a chance to step away from working and have a moment in the backroom to process everything. I had advice from my co-workers to dump all her belongings outside and tell her to get lost. Others told me to move out of my apartment before she got back from her trip. My feelings were everywhere, so I didn't know what to say or do. That night, I decided that I would confront her about it in person once she got back from Michigan, totally catch her off guard, and make her realize I found out. The very last element of this plan is that I would record the audio of our conversation. I live in a time where men get accused all the time of accusations, and I didn't have any evidence of her cheating other than her text messages, and I didn't have access to those. My only chance of getting solid evidence was having a voice recording of her admitting or reacting to cheating.

Three days after she left, she had a return flight back to New York. I waited in the living room for her as I knew she was coming home later that night. I explained to our other roommate, who we shared the apartment with, to keep out of the living room since I knew things would get messy. The stage was set. I heard my "girlfriend" walking up the stairs outside, I pressed record on my cell phone, and put it facing down on the coffee table in the center of the room. She turned the doorknob and entered the living room. I swallowed my ego and emotions for ten minutes and asked her about Michigan. She showed me photos of her mom and our old dog that we had to give away before leaving for New York. She felt so happy to have visited family and friends. Once she hopped up from the couch and opened the fridge, I knew she had no fucking clue I had found out, and that's when I decided it was time to drop the bomb on her.

"Hey last Friday when you said you were going to have a girl's night, did you REALLY have a girl's night?"

She just stared into the fridge and took a second to respond.

"Yeah, I did."

I looked at her and asked again.

"I'm gonna ask you one more time, last Friday, did you actually have a girl's night?"

She struggled to analyze the situation, and asked me what game I was playing.

That's when I unloaded it on her. She closed the fridge as if her hunger dissipated into thin air. All she could do was ask how I found out, but I never gave her that answer. I explained my anger and frustration to her, I told her there were multiple moments where I wanted to throw all her shit off the balcony while she was in Michigan. My trust in her was completely gone. How could I trust people now that she had back-stabbed me like this? She responded with this state-ment,

"I don't know what to tell you, I don't know- I... I've... I don't know. I have a lot of problems, and I've had a lot of problems my whole life, and I've always been a liar, and I've always been a cheater and I've done this and... this is how it goes. Maybe you have a little pity for my last boyfriend, maybe you have a lit-tle pity for... all these other dudes, because this is not- you're not the first person."

Boom. I had the statement secured in the bag. I told her that she could stay here in the apartment, but she would have to sleep in the living room. She told me that she would leave tonight. She headed for our bedroom and I followed her, just to make sure she wouldn't destroy any of my belongings on her way out. She opened the closet and started grabbing clothes, it's as if she choreographed this because she was packing pretty fast. The only reason I remember this part of the story is because she struggled to reach for a briefcase that was at the top shelf of our closet, and she angrily asked for my help. I got up and reached for her suitcase, as I pulled her luggage out from the top of the closet, a folded sleeping bag started to fall off the same shelf and I caught it with my hand. I looked over to her and asked if she would be needing this as well, she didn't like that statement and yelled quite loud at me.

Before she left, she told me that I should look at the "bright side" and realize that now I could be with anyone in this city. I told her that my trust in dating was broken and that I will probably be by myself for a long time. I had numerous chances later on down the road to date other people I had met or through dating apps like Tinder, but I always couldn't pull the trigger and put my faith into being vulnerable again and trusting someone else. Living with a cheater was a miserable experience because the damage she did lasted longer than she'll ever know.

I'll end this story by saying this, if you no longer want to be with somebody you are dating and wish to sleep or fool around with other people, please talk to your partner and break up with them before fucking somebody else behind their back. It might not hurt you if you cheat behind your partner's back, but you'll destroy any trust your partner can form with other people in the future if they ever find out what you did to them. It would be nice to end this breakup story circling back to the poster she hung above our bed, but the sad thing is, there wasn't any love coming from her side of the relationship at the end, the only love that seemed to be torn apart was mine.

Getting By While High

Like most people, I don't remember much of me being a little kid. I swear, having consciousness hit me at the age of four or five when I was standing at a playground. Once I was three years old, my younger brother was born and thus I had always shared a room with him. Even when I moved out of my house at age 20, I shared a place with my girlfriend at the time, so when the breakup happened, I didn't have the money to pay for her side of the rent. This is when I moved to Brooklyn where I finally had a room to myself, with the only downside of sharing a kitchen and bathroom with random roommates. This living situation helped save money with the rent being split between us all. It was quite weird during this time because I was unable to trust anyone to a point where I would be capable of being in a relationship with them and New York was already an expensive city, so instead of spending my time in Manhattan where I would be forced to buy expensive food or have to pay for a coffee to use bathroom in any cafe, I spent most of my time hanging out in my room or on the public rooftop for the whole apartment building. For the first time, it felt good to be alone. I started to master the art of being content with just being by myself.

I luckily was able to use Starbucks to attend college for free online through their partnership with Arizona State University, no I'm serious, completely free. The company paid for the tuition in full which is mind-blowing since attending college in America costs you an arm and a leg. The only downside to attending university online is that there is not a way to make friends that you can hangout with in person. I was pretty lonely at times, only a handful of people were willing to spend time with me, but it was okay. Thankfully, I had online games to entertain me, and occasionally I would be able to play online with my brothers or friends who lived out of state. Luckily, I had roommates in the apartment I was living in. One of them was super chill, his name was George. He would always play vinyl records and mix with reggae music in the living room, and oftentimes he was high. He was the person who introduced me to weed.

I realized early in my life that I have an addictive personality when it comes to certain things, my first addiction was obviously video games, my second was caffeine. My parents love drinking coffee. They made me realize that drinking coffee every morning was a routine for most adults. I think if they ever end up in the hospital one day, they will request that their IV has coffee dripping inside their body. Working at Starbucks didn't help because I had access to any drink I wanted while I was working. Soon I realized that being hooked to coffee daily was horrible because on the off chance I didn't come in early enough to drink something before my shift started, I would be a walking angry zombie to everyone. Sometimes I wasn't in the mood to drink a pumpkin spice latte, so I told myself no, but later in the evening the headaches would hit me as a withdrawal symptom, and it was horrible. Two months into working at Starbucks, I decided that I wanted to quit drinking coffee because I didn't want to be addicted to caffeine anymore, but I just started drinking iced tea instead. Weeks later, I realized that my tea addiction was still a caffeine addiction, so I quit that too. I would wake up, go to work early in the morning, come home in the afternoon, and take a nap until dinner time. My body wasn't used to not having caffeine in its system so I was tired for a week straight, often napping in the middle of the day. After the withdrawal symptoms were gone, it felt good to be off of caffeine, but I had other problems. After my breakup, I drank alcohol a little too often.

The first week I was living in Brooklyn, my roommates took me out for drinks to celebrate me moving in. Quite a nice gesture to say the least, and thus we were out at a nearby pub drinking and just spending time with each other in February 2018. This is when George asked me if I had ever smoked weed before and I told him no.

"Well, if there was ever a day you were gonna try, I say tonight is the night you hit this joint Matt."

The household I grew up in always told me to stay away from drugs, and that they would only simply distract me and get me into trouble, however I had no mom or dad around, and for the first time I thought to myself, he's right. This is a new chapter in my life and I think I ought to try and relax and try smoking weed for the first time. After all, I was already halfway with being 21 years old, it's a late start compared to everyone else I knew who dabbled with weed as teenagers.

The very first couple of times I smoked weed, there wasn't a huge effect. Eventually, I smoked enough one evening with George to the point where playing Mario Kart in our living room turned into an extremely exciting and bright activity, but still the feeling drifted away quite quickly, and I was never good at rolling joints. I also didn't like the fact that I had to smoke something and put it in my lungs to get high. One thing I despise to the end of the earth is cigarettes, and even though smoking weed isn't the same smell as cigarettes, I still dread the feeling of inhaling smoke into my lungs because I know that it is something that harms my body, so I wasn't always thrilled to smoke weed due to my anxiety always constantly reminding me that what I am doing is bad for my health.

One evening I came home from work and explained to my roommate George that there was this art gallery that had a video game night. It's where they set up a bunch of projectors and TVs with video games consoles and the whole art gallery turns into a night where everyone can drink, smoke, and play video games with each other. I had gone the week before and drank too much with friends, so I was hoping to have a chill time going there with no alcohol. George was in the kitchen putting something in the oven, and he asked if he could come with me. I told him of course he could tag along. He mentioned that he had to wait some time before he could take his edibles out of the oven and then he would be ready to leave after they were done. He asked if I ever took edibles before, I said no. He generously offered me one and told me to be careful with how much I take, as it would hit me later on during the day.

I didn't think too much of it and swallowed a piece of the edible. I was quite happy to be able to take weed without having to smoke it, but I didn't feel high so perhaps nothing crazy would happen. I remember walking with George in the night towards this art gallery and started to feel slightly weird. Upon arriving at the art gallery, there were people and video games around so I didn't think much of how I was feeling, I just started to have fun. Suddenly, out of the blue, bam. This edible hit my bloodstream while I was in this dimly lit art gallery with nothing more than the video games projected on the walls to gaze at. This was the night I realized I liked taking weed as edibles way more than smoking it. It felt healthier and the feeling lasted longer when it came to the duration of feeling high. A week went by and I asked George for the recipe. He sent me a YouTube video by *Vice* called "How to Make Fire Cracker Edibles at Home". This video changed my life, as I started to get high often with edibles. I even got to a point where I read that if you ate mangos, you could get even higher. I'm no scientist, but the best way I can describe why is because whatever is inside the mangos that gets broken down when your body digests it, it amplifies the THC that is within weed edibles to make your high feel even more intense. My favorite part about weed is that it didn't give me a bad experience like alcohol did. With alcohol sometimes I would get sad if I drank certain drinks, or if I drank too much my food would leave my stomach, not the mention the next day waking up groggy. Weed was great. Sativa made me want to go walking all over the parks, Indica made me want to chill in my hammock on my rooftop, or play video games in my room. It was mind numbing and put me in a relaxed mood. Made my anxiety leave my body and everything was quite funny. Music felt extremely pleasant to listen to, and if I took a high enough dosage, my vision was slightly trippy to me.

I decided to quit drinking alcohol entirely at the end of June in 2018. I would only consume edibles as my go to drug. It came to a point where George got worried for me and advised that I shouldn't take weed so often. He explained that if I got high on a daily basis, my tolerance level would build up and I wouldn't be able to get as high as I wanted to. If I took some days off from taking any weed, it would successfully reset the tolerance build up I had in my body. He was right, I realized myself that I started to become a little bit too attached to being high on edibles as a method of distracting myself from adult life world.

During my days where I wasn't getting stoned, I accidentally stumbled into a rabbit hole about lysergic acid diethylamide, you might know this as LSD. I had a keen interest on acid, a drug that was fantasized to no other belief in the 1960s but soon was banned with no explanation as to why from the U.S. government. The topics I read online stated that it could change your life and it's not an addictive drug. Before attempting to try LSD, I figured I should baby step my way to it and try psilocybin mushrooms first. These too are illegal, so it took some time to find somebody who sold them, but once I found some, I took it in Central Park with my friend so I wouldn't experience my mushroom trip solo. I made sure to take small portions and not overdo it, as I had a friend back in Michigan who told me he would never touch mushrooms again after taking some at a party and having a horrifying trip for eight hours straight. Shrooms were enjoyable and I didn't have any extreme hallucinations. My mind wandered as I laid on the blanket we had spread out in Central Park and I stared at the trees. I didn't feel like moving much due to my stomach struggling to digest this fungus, but the trip inside my mind felt quite pleasant. This trip made me realize that one day I wish to move out of New York City to have more nature within my surroundings. I felt quite happy while under the effects on mushrooms, though I'm pretty sure my first trip was close to a micro dose.

After experiencing shrooms that danced in my mind, I figured I was ready to take LSD. However, I told myself I wouldn't actively look for it, and once I accidentally ran into somebody who sold it, I would take it as a sign from the universe that it was my time to take it. Little did I know, a month after my shroom trip, as I sat in a tattoo chair getting more ink on my arm, another artist in the studio mentioned to me that she sold tabs. I finally had somebody who would sell me some "Lucy" but I realized that LSD could change my life. It was the only drug that activated your brain to work and communicate with more parts of itself at once. I took several days to think about it, looking up videos of people who had horrifying trips on LSD, reading how others had trips and it completely changed their life or helped them cure addictions they previously had. Other people stated that it changed their mindset to life forever once their trips were over.

My curiosity to what it could potentially do overcame me, and I found myself walking to this person's apartment on a warm August night in 2018. I paid for my tab and asked how I consume the drug properly.

"You just put it on your tongue and wait about an hour," they replied.

"Like this?" I asked as I put the tab on my tongue.

Her and her boyfriend's eyes widened. They wished me luck.

I had taken the tab at 8pm at night, and started walking back home. My thoughts echoed louder in my head as I waited for the acid to hit me like a baseball bat. Would my life change? Was this going to be a horrifying trip? Did I take something that is laced?

I remember walking home and a girl from tinder asked me if I would bring her coffee. All my friends were busy at the moment, and I wanted to have somebody close by in case my trip was intense, so I walked inside a bodega, bought a coffee, and headed to this girl's place. She was outside smoking a cigarette, which already was a turn off for me, but I wasn't here to be romantic, I was here to talk and have somebody else to listen to in hopes that it would distract me from my nervousness. We hung out outside her apartment steps as she sipped her coffee, and the warm summer air laid on my shoulders.

Eventually, I felt something, and I realized the trip was beginning. To be 100% honest with you, I can't explain an acid trip with words. If I were able to make the following words you are reading right now stand up, start dancing and wiggling in front of your eyes, then perhaps you'd understand what an LSD trip is, but I sadly can't do that, so you'll just have to use your imagination. I soon told this girl I had to leave, as I had too much energy in my body, and I thanked her for her time. She thanked me in return for the coffee and wished me luck. I remember walking around Brooklyn and just laughing and staring at everything that seemed interesting to me. Being on acid is like becoming a rabbit, you have the urge to bounce around everywhere and not sit in one place. Eventually, I walked around Brooklyn and woke my friends up who lived nearby, and they were able to spend time with me from two to five in the morning, asking me how my trip was and to have me paint or listen to music. LSD is quite an active drug, I had so much energy and was unable to fall asleep. I remember the trip was wearing off as the sun was coming up, and I was able to watch the sun rise from within my apartment, which is something I typically never see because I'm lazy and if I'm able to sleep in, I will.

LSD helped me realize that I should enjoy the small things within my life. It made me understand how precious and fragile I am as a human. The fact I am even alive at the moment is fucking crazy. Why do I have stress in a society where the government tells me I should go work jobs that I don't enjoy in return for money? I should also mention most of my paycheck goes to rent and food. This is when I realized why LSD was banned by the government. They tried to use it on soldiers in the military in an experiment in the 1960s hoping that they could make super soldiers who could be a bigger threat to enemies in wars in the future, but they soon realized the men wouldn't follow orders, and the results showed that people started to think more independently and didn't want to do things they had no interest in.

Acid changed my life entirely. I'm not saying this so that you can run out, lick 10 stamps and go crazy. I've already written about how an acid trip can go wrong. It can be overwhelming and can scare you if you are in a bad place in your life. One time, I took acid and walked around a museum, I got overwhelmed by the people inside the museum and how I felt trapped inside a building. I just remember having to sit down on a bench and drew in my journal for several minutes to calm my anxiety. Another acid trip I experienced is when I had an ego death, where I took two tabs and was alone by myself in Prospect Park. The end of the trip was fun, but during the peak it was extremely intense within my body, and I just stuttered words like crazy for two hours straight because I was alone and a nervous wreck. I remember calling my friends and family during this trip and just telling them I loved them and how I was quite happy to have them in my life. The phone call with my dad didn't go so well, he asked me if I was high and I told him yes. He said to me that he didn't want to talk to me while I was in this state and hung up the phone.

Strange that a drug which makes me feel good about life, if I take the right proportion of it of course, is banned to the public. I understand how if LSD falls in the wrong hands or if you take too much, you can head straight into bad situations, but on the other hand if taken in the right setting with the right people around to make sure you are okay, it did wonders to my life. I decided I wanted less possessions and that I wanted to experience events as well as see more places while I am still alive. It helped changed my eating behaviours for the better. Tripping on LSD always throws me the reminder that I am just a small little organism on a rock that is floating endlessly around a giant explosion of fire in space, and that always makes my problems feel less intense, I shouldn't take life insanely seriously.

Not everything is fun and daisies when you take drugs. Just like when you stop consuming coffee or cigarettes, your body experiences withdrawals and the same rules apply if you take weed or LSD. For acid, the withdrawals aren't as intense, since each trip is like a roller coaster ride, so you don't have the drive to keep taking more the following day. I only found myself being a little tired and having less energy the day after any trip I've had, since the day of each trip I would laugh a lot and walk around due to having too much energy from being high. Weed withdrawals are my guess as to why a lot of people find themselves depressed. Similar to acid, weed does the same thing where it releases a lot of dopamine into your brain, unlike acid where you might only trip once in a blue moon, weed is often times done regularly. Some people wake up and smoke weed several times a day. The day you go without weed, the withdrawals of being more sad, having less energy, and being easily annoyed hit you. It can last for several days too. I call this sadness withdrawal the "post weed depression" and it can make you feel like life is miserable. Often times it's why so many people who are addicted to weed end up falling back into it, due to knowing the quickest cure to "post weed depression" is simply getting high.

It's a horrible cycle to be trapped in, and I found myself dealing with this along with being lonely. Starbucks ended up giving us six free therapy sessions, as they realized a lot of their employees ended up dealing with mental health issues, I took advantage of it and went to a therapist in the fall of 2018. I'm quite fearful of taking antidepressants after seeing a friend of mine who took them and just looked like a numb person who was incapable of showing any emotions. I told my therapist it was a harsh no for antidepressants. She advised me after the six free sessions that I needed more appointments with her to make more progress, however I was unable to pay for it. I already was making little money having to pay for rent, phone bill, groceries, and my weed addiction. I didn't have an extra $200 a week for therapy appointments. I remember she got angry that I wouldn't have a way of returning, and advised me to ask others to help me pay for it, but I knew nobody would come to my aid. My parents were already disappointed I was taking drugs, and thus any extra money I could ask them for, they would simply think it would go towards weed.

I was getting tired of working a job in the city where I made caffeine drinks for people, which is just a legalized drug for everyone in society, and yet I was shunned upon for consuming weed and LSD that is illegal in the government's eyes. Tons of people walk into Starbucks being cranky and not wanting to talk or be friendly until they have their first sip of coffee, but that withdrawal is normal and okay to have. However, me being depressed because I'm not high at work is a personal issue that I have to handle and take care of.

Life simply didn't seem fair in my eyes, and I was not happy at all with where I was. I came to New York to become an actor, and yet there I was slaving myself at a coffee shop and getting high in the evenings. Yikes. It hit me that I was in a bad place when I found myself not eating food in the morning because I realized that if I took an edible on an empty stomach, the high would be more extreme than normal. I was simply getting by while high. I felt a little unmotivated to do anything or change, since my rhythm was comfortable for me. The only thing I looked forward to was the release of *Star Wars Episode IX*. I decided that after I saw that movie, I would have nothing else to live for, other than taking weed daily and LSD every other month until the day I die.

Jiggly

As a kid, my father showed me and my siblings the *Star Wars* films. He grew up seeing episodes four, five, and six in the late 70s and 80s. My brothers and I would often be found outside swinging lightsaber toys at each other and pretending we had the force to push and electrify our foes. I was stoked when I heard they were making new *Star Wars* movies and it made me excited to keep living my life, even though I was in a depressed state due to being alone, dealing with a drug addiction, and trying my best to live in an awfully expensive city.

First showing of the film would premiere the night of December 18th, 2019. I ended up filming a video and publishing it on YouTube called "it's okay to be alone but sometimes it sucks." In the video I showed my frustration on camera and how I was sad about being alone. I discussed about death and how each of us as people end up in the ground and there is no evidence that nothing happens to us post death, we could just die and that's it. Black screen. You can tell in the video it bothers me slightly and I don't know how to take it. I ended up going outside with an edible in my system, walking around a graveyard, and filmed a couple of my thoughts. That's it.

I figured if I was going to die because of depression, I might as well have a hint on my YouTube channel that showed people how I was feeling before it happened. I edited the video the day Star Wars came out and published it. I went straight to the movie theaters after uploading my video. I sat down in the theater with a packed audience. A guy next to me asked if I was excited and I said yes. We shared our anticipation with one another. I asked him what his name was.

"Luke." he replied.

Crazy that I am sitting in theaters for a new *Star Wars* movie and the person next to me happens to be named Luke. What a coincidence. Anywho, the film starts and I watch the movie. It was good, not the best *Star Wars* film but it took my attention away from the real world for over two hours, so I say it's a success. When the credits started to roll, I turned to Luke and asked him if he enjoyed the film. He said that it was good. I started gathering my trash and realized there was just one aspect missing before I left the theater.

"Luke. May the force be with you." I say on my way out.

He laughs and wishes the same to me. I end up making my way home and realized that I was no longer looking forward to anything now. Winter officially starts around the corner but it's already cold, so my mental health is already pretty deprived.

I messaged a girl on tinder about maybe hanging out with me, but she already bailed two times. I had nothing else going on with my evening, so I invited her over to hangout after I saw the film, however I knew the chances of her not coming over was high due to her previous times of saying no to hanging out. To my surprise, I heard a knock on my door minutes later.

I open it and see a girl standing there with dreadlocks. Now before I got on, I had told my co-workers at Starbucks that all alternative style girls with dreadlocks seem to be in Europe. I'm not sure if it's because Europe has a more open environment when it comes to expressing yourself, but in America it seems there are some things people are scared to do, especially like having dreadlocks as a white person. After browsing Instagram dreadlock pages, I found a lot of hippie girls with dreadlocks happen to be found in Germany. I told my co-workers often that the very first girl I found that would fit this stereotype, she would be the woman of my dreams, no doubt. Now obviously it was said as a joke, mostly because I had frustration that I couldn't find hippie like-minded people in New York, but I wasn't surprised because hippie people don't want to live in expensive cities. Somehow, when I opened the door, it seemed to be an exact version of a human that I had previously spoken out, everything except she probably wasn't German, since no tourists would be in New York close to the Christmas holiday.

She came into my apartment and I asked her if she wanted anything to drink, she said tea. Now I didn't drink much other than water and occasionally orange juice, so I had no kettle to warm up water. How do you think I warmed up her tea? I put water in a mug with her teabag inside and put it in the microwave. That's right, microwave. I'm bachelor status right here ladies. Line up. Anywho, I sat with her in my kitchen and after the first ten minutes, I found out that she was in fact from Germany. I thought for a second reality was pulling a prank on me, because this seemed too accurate to what I joked would be my dream girl to my co-workers. Most of my tinder dates I had typically played out with me going on dates with someone for two weeks and then realizing I disliked who they were, or they disliked who I was, and then it would be back to the drawing board. With this girl, I decided to do a speed round of questions to make sure she is somebody I might like.

I learned her name was Salome. She was by herself in America doing a work study at a psychiatric center where she does art therapy with patients. I had no idea what art therapy was, so she explained it to me. I couldn't believe she was in America by herself, I found we were similar in that we were both in the big apple on our own solo adventures and had no fear if something happened to us because we both knew that we would be the ones to get us out of any situation we fell in. I also realized since she was working in art therapy that she was smart because she has a good understanding of how people behave with her studies in art therapy. I asked her if she believed in a god and she stated that she didn't, but perhaps there is more out there, such as the universe itself that is the reason as to why we are here.

I like Salome a lot. She's smart, adventurous, and not afraid to go to a boy's house in Brooklyn on a cold December night. We started spending any free time we had with each other. I showed her all the cool places I adventured to by myself and hoped she would like it. Brooklyn Bridge, Williamsburg, Highland Park, Caffeine Underground, Columbus Circle, Evergreen cemetery and many other places. It was crazy because the day before I met her, I filmed a YouTube video stating that I was lonely and frustrated. The same day I edited and posted that video was the exact day she knocked on my door. It's like I spoke out to the universe that I needed something, wished for change, and it came directly to me. I am so thankful.

After many weeks of getting to know Salome, I realized that I may be in love with her. She is somebody I want to spend every day with because of her actions and stories. The tales she told of each country she had visited made me realize she was brave for jumping into new experiences. Her struggles with communication in English and not knowing what words to use made me smile often. Salome has the biggest heart in the world when it comes to helping other people. One time somebody on the subway train was showing signs of being sick, and everyone stepped away from this person in fear of getting sick themselves, I was one of them. Salome was the only person to walk over to this sick passenger and offer them her bottle of water since they looked like they needed help. Salome was living in an Airbnb sharing a small apartment room with two other foreigners. I told her she could move in with me, as her living situation was rough and I wanted to spend more time with her.

During the next two months before she had to leave for Germany, we explored museums, went dancing, ate different foods, spent days visiting tourist locations, and of course played games. One day we had some friends over and all of us were playing the video game *Super Smash Bros*. My roommate George came home and saw the vibe. He wanted to join our game. We hooked up a controller for him and he had to pick a character.

"Hmm... I think I'm gonna be Jigglypuff."

He put his token on Jigglypuff's icon and the announcer shouted the name "Jigglypuff" out from the television speakers. A few rounds were fought as George from Jigglypuff and during the middle of a round, he handed the controller to me and said he needed me to finish the fight. Being the pro gamer that I am, I whooped everyone else in that match with Jigglypuff. However, little did we know that Salome's brain would echo this name in her head for the next several days, until it slipped out of her mouth

"Jiggly. Jiggs." She called out in her adorable little voice with a slight accent.

I turned to her and laughed. The days following she nicknamed me jiggs and my head would always face her once that name was spoken. Even to this day, we still call each other Jiggly or Jiggs, and it's all because my roommate George decided to play the *Pokémon* character of Jigglypuff in *Super Smash Bros.* that one evening.

I asked her if she was willing to stay in New York City for another six months because then I would be able to complete my degree. Once I would graduate, I told her that I would move to Germany with her. Salome liked this plan since she wanted to stay with me as well, so our plan was set. She'd get a job in the city to have money come in to afford living expenses. However, we soon ran into a problem where she realized she wouldn't be able to extend her visa. One day I came home from work and found her on the rooftop. She told me how it was impossible for her to stay and that she would have to leave once her visa expired in the beginning of March 2020. I looked at her, and then looked at the cityscape behind me. I realized how empty my life would be without her around, and that I wouldn't want to spend another second in this city without this other human being. I looked directly at Salome and told her that I was hoping I could wait till a later date to say this, as it seemed too early to say it, but it seemed important to hear.

"I love you."

I told her that I didn't care about graduating and getting a degree, and that I would drop it all if it meant I could be with her. I wish you could've seen her face, because it's one of the happiest moments I've had in my life. Legit felt like a movie. The sun was going down, wind blew occasionally to add that dynamic rooftop aura into our minds, and the city lights were turning on in the background. She said those three words back at me, and the preparation for getting a passport processed as well as packing up my apartment had begun.

It's crazy because I had known Salome for 24 days, and now it was decided I would move to Germany with her. Maybe I'm impulsive and follow my heart but that's the only way I want to live. I'd be heartbroken if I would have to say goodbye to her, and I wasn't able to go through that. Who cares if I didn't graduate from college, it may suck because I have no clue when I will be able to see my friends or family again, but my heart told me I couldn't be without Salome.

We packed up my apartment over the next month, and soon we were ready to head towards Deutschland. It was also a huge turning point for me because this would be the very first time I would leave America. I've lived both on the west and east coast, but I've never experienced life in a different country. None of my friends or family would be anywhere close to me, in fact, a giant ocean would be between me and everyone I knew and loved, not to mention a language barrier would also be an obstacle I would have to overcome. Nevertheless, I didn't feel any fear inside. Salome made me feel so comfortable with her, and I trusted her with all my heart. It felt good to finally be able to be vulnerable with somebody again, it's scary too, but once I let go with the right person, it feels incredible. I think using the word incredible to describe love doesn't do it any justice. Just look around at how many songs that are sung, movies that are filmed, or books that are written that all have love as a main topic. Obviously, having love in your life is a big deal for us humans, but it's nothing we can buy or find when we want it. Sometimes you just have to wait until it arrives at your door on a December cold night, I'm just thankful that she is in my life.

Before leaving, I remember a photographer contacted me and asked for a day to shoot some photos of me. I mentioned that I would be leaving March 1st, 2020, with a late flight heading straight to Europe, so during the day, I met with Robbie Quinn in Manhattan, where he photographed me for his book *Street Unicorns*. The book features people who dress or look differently than the typical human you would see on the street.

This is the last photo of me in New York City. After taking the photos, he asked me for a statement as to why I look this way.

Photo Credit Photographer Robbie Quinn

"I hope I'm a person that makes others smile. I want my look to pop out and help people to not take life so seriously. I feel being colorful can offer a distraction for others to forget for a second the problems of the world and that everything is a huge shit show. Life is extremely short. I want to dance to music I like, laugh at life's wonderful joys and have as much fun as possible - because we have no idea when our life has it's 'game over.'"

After this photo session, I headed back to Brooklyn, packed the last of my belongings, and headed straight to the airport with Salome. I remember the time was weird because a quarter of the people standing in line were wearing face masks and the others weren't. There was talk about a disease spreading around the world, but nobody seemed to be panicking. Luckily, I had a facemask I used when I would spray paint on the rooftop of my apartment. I remember wearing that mask in the airport as I was a little skeptical about what was going on. I had no idea that the timing of leaving New York couldn't be better because the COVID-19 Pandemic was right at America's doorstep.

Die Welt War Ruhig

Euros look like monopoly money. This was the first thing I remember thinking about when it spit out of an ATM. The different colors and big numbers written on them instantly made my mind jump to the time of seeing the resemblance to the board game I played as a child. Also, side note, trying to find vegan food in airports is ridiculous, especially if you are in a country that doesn't speak your native language. Regardless, we made it to Germany, and I was excited to start exploring the country a bit more. I remember learning many things about Germany in my history classes in school. Topics like World War II and the Berlin Wall were covered, so I couldn't wait to find out new things about this place that holds an enormous amount of history within its borders.

One day we visited the city of Stuttgart to meet up with some of her friends. We decided that we should stop by the grocery store to get some stuff to cook for dinner. We walked through the store and found the banana section was completely gone. Not a single nana sitting on the shelf. It was strange to say the least. We continued browsing the store and realized all the toilet paper was whipped off the shelves too. Very weird. That's when this pandemic started to hit me hard, perhaps this was going to be a big deal. The very last location we got to see before the pandemic started was a castle in Baden-Württemberg. We got a look inside the castle and learned how people who had money back in the day got to live. This is when I realized there are older history landmarks in Germany compared to America, since American landmarks started appearing in the 1700s. Right when I felt like exploring Germany was just getting started, it soon came to a halt one day when the country announced it was going under lockdown due to a disease called COVID-19 that had infected more areas than they had predicted. After hearing this news, I remember Salome's dad stopped by our house to drop off groceries for us.

"You stay inside. Don't leave the house. If you need something, you can call me." he advised us after handing over toilet paper, which seemed to be a rare necessity in March 2020.

I remember calling my family and explaining the situation with them. Everybody was clueless of how big of a deal this pandemic would affect everybody in every single corner of the world. In a way, it made me feel more comfortable that even my family in America was dealing with the same problems I was facing here in Germany. Salome and I logged a lot of hours into video games like *Fortnite* and *Animal Crossing* during quarantine. Not gonna lie, she got really good at building and shooting other online players in *Fortnite*, we had endless time to get victory royales, to the point where we even got her father to start jumping out of the battle bus with us. We went about a week straight without leaving the house, but eventually we wanted some fresh air. Salome and I stepped outside and took a walk around the neighborhood.

I've never heard the silence of no cars driving around like this before. Salo decided to take a ukulele outside with her and strummed the strings on it as we walked around the outskirts of the city. Complete silence, not even a vehicle passed by us as we ventured around. Only the echoes of the ukulele filled the air, which is quite a relaxing sound to hear, but in the eeriness of the massive silence in the world around us, it seemed much louder compared to her small fingers that flung on the wooden instrument. Die welt war ruhig, or to those who speak English, that phrase translates to "the world was quiet", and indeed it was during the first lockdown. This was a true test for our relationship, as we were trapped inside with one another for a long time. Even though it may sound like a recipe for disaster to spend loads of time with another person for days on end, Salome and I love spending time with each other. We binged movies, played more games, took walks, and just waited until things would hopefully change. I was thankful to realize that we didn't get sick of one another.

This pandemic helped me learn a lot about humans and how fragile our society is. Quite frankly, the example of essentials in grocery stores flying off the shelves for days is evidence that our foundation of living can easily be broken and fall apart within a matter of time. All it takes is fear mongering and people go crazy. We as humans sometimes have giant egos, and this pandemic did a good job to remind me that sometimes in life we never know when the end game will come directly at us. I was lucky enough to be with somebody I really cared about, and I just thought I should keep enjoying each day that enters my life because my heart could stop beating tomorrow for all I know. I like to think that my ego was tamed due to this pandemic, but it seems a lot of people haven't followed in my footsteps. There are lots of people who would walk around without masks on, which to me felt like a straight disrespect to those who had already died or had friends or family members die because of the virus. I understand everyone believes in different ways of living their life, but I thought this example of seeing humans not wearing their masks in public made me realize that some people don't care for others. It's a bit sad. Dumb people like this give me anxiety about going out in public and talking to anyone. To this day, I still have a voice in my head when groups of people approach me and begin talking without their mask on. I understand that I'm young and have a good chance of surviving COVID-19, but I'm not gonna chance going through being sick, and potentially losing my sense of smell or taste afterwards.

Another thing that bugs me with this pandemic is that everyone was rushing to get their vaccine. I understand y'all want to have fun and go to festivals, theme parks, or go shopping. To me, the government hasn't done a single thing to make me trust them more. In fact, this pandemic has shown that with how greedy they were to even attempt to hand money out to those in need and how little they gave to small businesses who struggled gives me even more evidence as to why I believe the government isn't there to protect or help me. I think the government doesn't give a flying fuck about my ass. They wouldn't bat an eye if they found me dead on the sidewalk one morning. Naturally, when the government starts telling everyone left and right to get the vaccine, which was something that was developed very quickly within a year, I start to have suspicions. My very first problem is that the vaccine could have dangerous side effects in the long term. The data in the world obviously shows that people aren't growing third arms or turning into zombies when they get stabbed with the needle, but we have no idea what these things will do to us in the long run of five or seven years. The data pool is empty in that area. It's just like when doctors back in the day told people who were sick to smoke cigarettes, then they realized 30 years later that people were dying from lung cancer.

Don't get me wrong, the vaccine could be helpful and could end this pandemic for good, but since most vaccines they test for several years before pushing it out to the public, and yet this one they rushed out the door as soon as possible, it makes me extremely nervous to get it done because quite frankly, I don't have any drive to be a lab rat for the government. I have nothing against people who have already gotten the vaccine, but I do have a problem with those who taunt and make a big deal towards others who don't get the vaccine. It's fucking annoying. Suddenly I'm a bad person to those who are vaccinated because I'm not repping the government on my t-shirt and standing in line to get my arm stabbed. I take more responsibility to always leave my apartment with my mask on even more now because currently I am not vaccinated.

It doesn't help my decision of getting the vaccine when I know a lot of money from Bill Gates was dumped into helping companies create these vaccines, even though years before the pandemic happened, he talked about how the earth is overpopulated. Things like this make me think twice before wanting to sign up for a vaccine that may have a side effect of making humans infertile in the long run, but again because the data isn't there yet, I'm still undecided on how I feel. What makes me angry is that the government is making it more difficult for those who haven't willingly gotten their vaccine. Travel is harder to do now without it, benefits are kept from those who choose to not get the needle, and other various forms of tactics that the government is using to try and push its people in the corner to get vaccinated. That shit isn't cool whatsoever. To anyone who hasn't gotten the vaccine, please be extra careful. I'm already a nervous wreck when it comes to getting sick, but we all should be more cautious in this whole mess we are going through, even if you don't enjoy wearing a mask or you're angry that you can't live life like it was before, boo hoo. Grow up. If you haven't learned the harsh reality yet, I'll slap it in your face, life is always changing and will never stay the same. Enjoy each day's colors, because tomorrow a new color palette is likely to be put on.

Sadly, the stress of the pandemic had an effect on my mental health. I started picking back up on my usage of edibles whenever I was able to find people who sold marijuana to me. The year 2020 was a time period of excessive edible consumption for me, and after several months, Salome confronted me about the issue and asked if I could take less. It made me open my eyes up and realized that I could slow my usage, and I did. However, I was still taking edibles every weekend, which that consumption rate was still an addiction in a mild level. She sat me down and talked to me again about the situation.

"Do you really want to live your whole life having to rely on this plant for happiness and escapism?"

That sentence hit me hard. I guess I felt bad for myself when I found out that I was more happy while high compared to when I was sober, and that was a bad sign. When it comes to drugs, I understand people will take them in order to feel good. Hopefully, you aren't somebody who is taking hard drugs, but I know people enjoy sipping coffee, smoking a joint, drinking a beer with friends, etc. However, if this is something you rely on daily and you catch yourself taking your choice of drug alone, I highly advise rethinking how often you take it and see if you can challenge yourself to consume less. I went cold turkey on edible usage in January 2021. I felt like I could only last a month and I would be back on it, but as I write this piece in June 2021, I've been off of weed edibles since the beginning of the year. Crazy right? I've come a long way of bingeing edibles daily during some parts of my life, to now being able to wake up and not have any thoughts or temptations in my head. Does this mean I will be sober forever? Who knows, but I'll definitely be more aware of how often I take something in my life. I wish that I will never fall back in that place of being hooked on taking something on a day-to-day basis.

Every day I wake up being thankful that Salome and I are healthy. I must remind myself that the current time we live in is a giant historical period and that I'm sure in several years it will be a whole subject in school where classes will study and discuss what happened to the world during the Corona outbreak for several weeks, and they'll probably take tests on the material. Just a little weird to be living in a huge moment within society where the rules are being changed daily. It's like somebody is rewriting the game's code as you are playing it. If you saw somebody wearing a mask in public in 2019, you would've thought it was weird and strange that they do this. Now it's accepted that everyone's mouths are covered while they are out in public, and we don't think twice about it. What a bizarre time it's been, and if you have made it this far, pat yourself on the back. I'm sure it wasn't easy either. Lots of people had money struggles, have had friends or family members who got the virus, or maybe you even had COVID-19 in your body. Regardless of the traumatic and tough times it's been, I believe the worst is behind us.

Even though employment was tough to find in Germany, with the pandemic happening and a language barrier to get over, I ended up finding myself employed at a youth house. Soon I realized many young people who were forced to attend school online and didn't have the typical concerts or spots to hangout at anymore due to having to social distance, a majority of people who entered the youth house were struggling with their mental health. I too experienced troubled times in this pandemic, relying on weed to make me forget about my problems, and even struggled financially at times with money. Seeing everyone in similar situations helped me to realize that I wasn't alone in this bizarre time. Recently, I've been making mental health videos on YouTube to help get material out online for the youth house, as a way to educate young people on how to wiggle their way out of depression, anxiety, and other various mental illnesses, as well as reminding them that regardless of their age or gender, we all struggle with mental health.

To whoever is reading this book right now, I hope this pandemic didn't squash your faith in the future. Yeah, it sucks ass to be living in a traumatic event, but you've come this far. I applaud you on that. Tomorrow might even be more challenging than today, or perhaps the sun will shine, and things will be better. Stay on your toes, keep your body hydrated, and talk to others if you need help. You gotta hit that age where you're old and you get to tell all your grandkids of how much of a bad ass you were and how you survived a global pandemic.

Cell Phones As Pacifiers

The goal was simple, for me to be able to play *Farmville*. I realized that I needed to make an account on Facebook, and this was my entrance into the social media world in 2009. Before joining any of these networks where I could connect and message with anyone, in order to contact my friends and talk with them while we played the same games on the computer, I would often call them on my parent's household landline. Cell phones were new and expensive, and you'd have to pay for each minute you used when calling somebody. Boy we sure came a long way since then, because now if you check nearby, you probably have a cell phone within your general vicinity. Heck, you might even be reading this book on an electronic device which proves my point even more. I can't believe how impactful technology has become in our lives.

My parents have footage of us as babies and kids on old video cameras. Sadly, my father didn't have unlimited tapes he could use to film my life, but nevertheless there are examples of how technology was back in 1996 and the early 2000s from simply seeing me on camera. Now I can have half a terabyte in my pocket, and once that storage on my phone is full, I can dump all my files on a cloud, and then delete everything to make room for more space. It hit me like a truck that technology was advancing rapidly when I started seeing new game consoles get released with improved graphics, online compatibility, and various apps to use to be able to stream videos or download extra content for my games. I remember the very first day I got a phone that had a flip out full keyboard and a camera. Those were the days. I felt like a teenager who had his life complete when I flipped open my phone and had a keyboard to mash out text messages to communicate with friends or flirt with girls. Now we have a small computer in our pocket, and it's great. I can do whatever I want to with my little handy dandy cell phone, but is that actually a good thing to have? Do you really think our brains are meant to handle the constant beeps and boops that ring every time we get a notification? Absolutely not. In fact, our brains are frazzled and over stimulated because of these small devices. Humans are not meant to be harassed by technology on a daily basis like this, let alone staring into a phone screen for several hours.

After watching a documentary last year called *The Social Dilemma* on Netflix, which is about how our brains are affected by our phones, I turned off a majority of my notifications for any applications I have downloaded. The only ones I leave on are texting apps I use to contact family or friends and my email alerts for work are left on. All my social media, random phone games, and other useless apps that just consume my time are muted. To be honest, it's great to have less noise coming from my phone. Sometimes I do receive messages on these other apps, but because my phone isn't always going off, I'm not bothered to check them. In fact, I thought about one day getting rid of my smartphone and just switching to a flip phone, but the convenience of having a camera to take photos or film events with, a navigation system while I travel, and easy access to my banking account, it's harder than you think to throw away my rectangular shaped electronic device in the trash. In all honesty, I have adjusted to the conveniences of life by owning a smartphone, and this makes going a step back and trying to live without it extremely difficult. I'd be giving up applications I use that make my day-to-day life easier and less exhausting. I've had days where I thought about deleting everything, wiping my whole trail of activity off the internet, and just moving to a remote country and living my life off the land. However, I do like the internet, and having access to a working fridge along with heat and clean water is something that makes living more comfortable, so I haven't done this. Maybe one day I'll be able to know how to grow my own food and learn to live without society's comforts, but that's a long-term goal I have yet to achieve.

What's crazy is that these companies develop these apps to make us more hooked to stay on our phones. The algorithms that are created to learn our likes and interests without us specifically voicing what we like is incredible to witness. On one side of the spectrum, it's great to open up Netflix, YouTube, Instagram or any other app where we can binge media and see the interests that we like on our electronic home screens. It's quite a pleasant sight to see. The ease of access of being able to find videos on gaming or memes about New York that make me laugh is as simple as pressing a square icon on my phone. This kind of easy access to entertainment is fantastic. Each video I click on, and every piece of content that I choose to interact with affects the algorithm and what it will feed me in the future. If you have Instagram, go ahead and go to the discover section on your phone. You can access this page by pressing the magnifying glass icon, which should be in the bottom left corner close to the house icon where we typically spend our time scrolling and see what kind of content appears for you. Think about what kinds of media fills the squares on your discover page. For me its video games, dreadlocks, memes, and clips from films. There wasn't a single thing I filled out to Instagram to let them know that these are things I like. Based on what content I have interacted with or how long I looked at a photo or video, the algorithm adapts and changes itself to try and send content it thinks I will enjoy next. This process never stopped, and what happily began as an adventure to attend my virtual crops and animals inside the farm game within Facebook, it sadly had turned into a website that I started to catch myself scrolling on to entertain and numb my brain for hours a day. Seems like most people use cell phones as pacifiers to pass the time and ignore their thoughts.

First reason I always remind myself to put my phone down is that everyone online is putting on an image. We have no idea what company will come by and browse our lives and judge us based on what photos or videos we put to the public. Everyone is essentially wearing a mask on their social media unless you take photos of yourself taking a shit on the toilet. If you're not doing that, then I think you too are somebody who filters and chooses specific photos of what you want to have of yourself online. Makes sense though, we feel good seeing posts or highlights of our lives, and we like seeing other people doing well in their lives, but to go to an extent to not share media and posts that represent all spectrums of us, we don't paint realistic pictures of ourselves. From happy moments in our life that seems to get spread like butter online, and the rough patches we seem to hide away from everyone, we choose to spoon feed all the other users online this finely chiseled and detailed sculpture of ourselves that in the front may look pretty, but behind we are torn up and battered from any other angle you might look at us.

If I can trick my brain into believing the content online is genuine and good, eventually I'll walk away from social media due to the second factor of it being endless. Sometimes when I go to the movies and eat popcorn, I get a little sad when the bottom of the bucket becomes visible. It's annoying to have to get up and head to the concession stand to get a refill and potentially miss parts of the movie, but somehow the developers of these apps know that when it comes to social media, if your feed never stops, more than likely you'll chow down on that content for longer. These apps make it easy to waste time scrolling and browsing forever. It's exactly like my popcorn bucket in the movie theater, only it's a bucket that consists of endless black holes filled with content to shove down my throat. The anticipation of knowing the next scroll I do could have content that is quite interesting to watch, but it's simply a toxic relationship. Since we can keep scrolling and it keeps giving us media directly pointed into our faces, with every finger swipe on our screen more videos, photos, and memes magically appear while keeping our brains occupied. The more time we spend on the internet, which is a finely coded and planned out environment, eventually it will affect our brains. Models who have posts on Instagram that are edited to the point where you can't find a single flaw on their skin, politicians sharing stories that are negative in hopes that you will stay active and argue with other opposing beliefs in the comments section, and all the other tactics and tricks these apps use to keep us sucked into these worlds makes us run into assumptions that we as people aren't as beautiful, successful, or as hopeful in the future with our lives as we should be.

Since we are not paying to access these social apps, how do they get money? Well, directly from us without telling it to our faces. Go ahead and open any social media application and scroll for 30 seconds. How many ads did you see? For Instagram it's usually after every two or three posts. You can tell it's an ad since it states very "clearly" below the brand's name in small gray text, you'll see the word "Sponsored" appear. This explains that this company paid money to get a front row seat in front of your attention. What about advertisements we don't know about that are secretly placed in front of our vision? With influencers posing with products and looking the happiest they have been while coincidentally holding whatever product they want to sell to us in their hands, entrepreneurs trying to swindle us into spending money on their classes that promises that eventually we'll be able to make it big, or other random crap that we see online that is simply trying to rinse our wallets of every cent we have. I'm sad that what started as an application that I could scroll on to see what my friends are doing has turned into a shopping mall. Depressing to say that capitalism will always try to find a way to sneak into our lives.

Isn't it ironic that most viral posts online can typically be labeled under negative or content that can make you feel angry at the world? I can't remember the last time I saw a post about a kitten being rescued from a tree, but oh boy, you can find boat loads of content that are about politicians arguing, school shootings, and all this other negative stories that make you depressed. We should be told when shit hits the fan and social media allows us to spread news like wildfire when things need to be heard. However, do we really need to have our whole plate of food be a pile of trash? Mentally it drains me to hear about how many covid deaths happen each day, the conflicts in other countries who are killing each other over land or power, and governments creating laws that make it harder for people who are already struggling to make a living.

Maybe it's always been like this, and I was oblivious to the fact because I was too busy trying to get five other friends to join *Farmville* so that I can get a pink cow to put on my virtual farm, but now I realize that negative media is the kind of content that spreads fast. Seems like a lot of news media outlets realize this and a large majority of their content is stuff that simply makes you want to yell in all caps in the comments section. The world has problems, yes society isn't perfect, and I agree that we should always inform everyone with what it is going on, but sometimes I wish there was a blindfold button I could click on that gives me the ability to skip past the real life bullshit online. Guess it's my own fault to try to find comfort and relaxation on social media apps that have no boundaries of determining what goes viral and what will end up on the front page of your feed. In a way, this wild west aspect of social media is cool, but also there are headlines I read and videos I see that make me lose faith in humanity as a whole. Global warming is a huge problem, government corruption being controlled by the wealthy, and healthcare being treated as a business first and a commodity for its people last are just a handful of issues I'd change in a heartbeat if I could.

Worst part is, I like social media. Makes me happy to log onto these applications and talk to my friends, see what my family is up to, and discover all sorts of new things happening around the world. There can be a wide variety of great experiences I can have on social media, but lately it's hard for me to realize it's good for my health. Sad thing is, in order to be independent and make money on my own, I have no choice but to advertise my skills and products to people through social media. It's the reason why so many people can grow their small businesses online like video editors, clothing companies, or even promote books that you write to make a living. I'm going to officially apologize to you now if you came across my social media of me promoting my book. If I could just live off the sunlight and water, I wouldn't use my voice at all, however a boy has to eat, and due to the society we live in, I have to use social media to support myself. Sometimes I need to look back at the days where the grass was greener and social media's problems didn't exist, no really the grass was more green, the farm I had on that silly Facebook game was extremely bright green and well-watered.

Veeonepew

If you ask my mom, she'll tell you that she always had to rewind the movie *Toy Story* for me as a kid. I would wake up, watch the film, ask my mom to rewind the VHS tape so I could watch it again, and repeat the process until I played with my toys, or simply fell asleep. Rinse and repeat, I did this process for several weeks. *Toy Story* was my go-to film to enjoy. When I was younger, I wanted to be an astronaut when I got older, just like Buzz Lightyear was in the film. The very first time I replicated somebody in my life was probably that space ranger. My parents had bought me these Buzz Lightyear pajamas that whenever I spread my arms open, green netting would spread open in the shape of wings, so I could pretend I had the ability to fly. I would do the whole "to infinity and beyond" scene and fly all around the house. With my trusty space robot named XR by my side, who was from the *Buzz Lightyear of Star Command* cartoon show, my surroundings turned into any planet I could imagine, and it only took a slap on my wrist to be able to fire pretend lasers at my enemies.

The next character I impersonated in my life was Mario. I couldn't grow a big brown mustache at the age of seven, but I was able to run around my house with a red hat on and a yellow cape that he used as a power up in one of the video games I played. It was quite fun to pretend to be that Italian plumber because anything I had on my mind pretty much faded away. From that moment until I took off my hat, I was Super Mario. I had to worry about stomping on imaginary goombas, finding a green dinosaur who could aid me in my adventure, and of course rescue the princess. Luckily, I had a younger brother who would happily play the role of Luigi, and with the occasional shouting of "Wa-hoo" we were able to jump into the make-believe world that was the mushroom kingdom.

What is funny about being a kid is that you are allowed to play dress up and pretend to be different things because you have this extraordinary imagination when you are young, which is a thing that fades away as you get older. To this very same day, I try to practice holding onto that ability but sometimes I fail to launch myself back into that imagination level. Nobody questions you for wanting to be somebody else as a kid, but once I started to get older, I would get questions for why I looked a certain way. The first comments that made me realize I replicated people was when I walked around school with "swooshy" hair. Justin Bieber made this hairstyle popular and it was all over magazines and TV. My only guess as to why I replicated this hairstyle was because of seeing how successful this other boy was, who was also similar to my age. It's not like I sang Bieber's songs in my free time, I think I just wanted to be liked and appreciated when I was in middle and high school, just like Bieber was adored by the public. Girls in my school would walk up to me and nickname me biebs, others simply flirted with me because I looked like their celebrity crush. It was kinda weird that this kind of attention only came because I replicated somebody's hair, but soon I realized that it had its benefits for trying to get people to notice me.

Soon after the Bieber phase, I met somebody in my improv group who I felt looked badass. He was captain of our improv team and he always wore his skinny jeans with a studded belt and he tucked the ends of his jeans into his combat boots. I found that I liked how he dressed and thought he looked like a cool dude. Soon I thought, why not replicate it? After all, I was already wearing skinny jeans on the daily, why not wear the combat boots I had sitting in my closet, throw on a studded belt, and tuck my pants into the boots? I came to school one day dressed like this, but other people in my improv team noticed the resemblance quite quickly. One of them came up to me after practice was over and asked why I was dressed like this. She stated that it was weird and that I should stop doing whatever it was. To me I thought I looked cool, but then I realized that I guess because of how similar it was, maybe she found it unsettling. It wasn't a normal thing people do, so if it made the improv members within my surroundings uncomfortable, I should stop, especially since I had to be around those people daily.

As humans we grow up and subconsciously start to pick up and like different things that we see in other people. Oftentimes we find ourselves styling our hair differently without even knowing the reason why. I didn't purposely try to look like Justin Bieber, it just happened accidentally overtime without me realizing it was my goal in the background of my brain. People do this in all sorts of things all the time. We replicate catch phrases or different words we hear from the people we spend time with. Perhaps you'll dress a little differently because of what you see other people wear on television or music videos. Maybe you start to change your hairstyle due to seeing a stranger on the subway with an interesting look. The world is full of people that replicate and mimic one another without admitting that they took their inspiration from someone else. Look at how there are hundreds of different companies producing their own smartphone after Apple had their recent success with the first iPhone reveal. I could pick and choose many different topics to provide evidence that we all do this as humans, but the easiest way to prove this kind of behavior exists is to look at yourself and ask where each part of your style originates from or question why you behave the way you do. Most of the time, you can find a handful of things that makes up your style that is actually inspired from other sources, whether it's people, advertisements, or movies as your inspiration.

I was even mimicking other people while I was playing games. In the video game *Guild Wars 2*, there is a main storyline you follow that has a plotline of gathering various people that come from different races and banding them together in order to take down a dragon that is terrorizing the world you play on. Throughout the story, you'll meet main characters from each race that stand out and reappear in different missions as you play. Each of them has their specific look with certain armors they wear, different kinds of color palettes chosen for their outfits, and the regular aspects like their facial features or hair color. I found it interesting to create avatars that look similar to these characters in the story. It was fun to roam around the game with other players eyeing me as I walked by or fought beside them. Sometimes I would try to type messages back to those players who wanted to chat, but I would stay in character. These other players who already shared interest in how similar my character was to the main recognizable one in game would get a message back from me of what I would assume this character would say back to them. The community in game seemed to react in a positive manner with my clones. It was entertaining for me to look at every aspect of the characters and try my best to sculpt another toon in their presence.

When I was in the big ole depression mood after my breakup, I had recently saw *Star Wars: The Last Jedi*, and in the film I witnessed the actor Adam Driver have a big anger scene in the movie with his hatred towards Luke Skywalker. I could relate a lot to his frustration in the film because of what had recently happened to me with my ex-girlfriend, and soon I found myself growing my hair out and dyeing it black, similar to how Kylo Ren looked in the movie. Replicating this *Star Wars* character helped me let go of my problems that I had for a second because my focus and concentration was spent trying to look like somebody else. Perhaps it's because I could relate to Kylo's emotions or maybe it's because I was living by myself, and I needed to change after going through such a big breakup. Either or, my dream of having black hair came true, as it was something I always wanted to do in my teenage years, but my mother always told me no.

If you ever owned a GameCube, you may have played the game *Paper Mario: The Thousand-Year Door*. In the game there is this character named Doopliss. He is this small ghost with scary red eyes showing through the white sheet he wears and on top of his head is a blue cone shaped party hat with red stars. Doopliss is responsible for shapeshifting villagers in a nearby town into pigs. Your mission is simple, head to his castle and put an end to his wrongful acts. It's quite easy to get to the castle, in fact it only takes less than 15 minutes to reach the location and fight Doopliss. Halfway during the fight, he looks at Mario, poofs away into nothing, and a second later he pops up as a purple shaped color of Mario. He seems to have the same attacks as Mario that he uses on you during the fight, like trying to jump on your head to deal damage, which is exactly what you can do as Mario. Soon after defeating him, the game announces you beat the chapter, however, instead of the game putting the camera back on Mario, who has now left the room, the game resumes with the camera on the purple Mario. He is laying on the ground unconscious, and after pressing the A button, the purple Mario jumps up to his feet. You soon realize that you are now this Mario, and that Doopliss has taken your identity and is now in the real body of Mario. He is able to run around causing trouble due to simply swapping places with you to reap the benefits of not getting caught in town only because everyone thinks that he is the real Mario.

As a child this game blew my mind. The developers even tricked me into thinking this chapter was over by saying you had beaten that level after the battle with Doopliss, but it wasn't. I had to figure out a way to fight him again and get Mario's real body back. This scene stuck around in my head and every time I mimicked somebody, I thought for a second there was this little bit of Doopliss in me that lived on. While in theatre, I realized that some actors used techniques such as method acting, where if they were cast in roles, they would act like their characters all the time, even off screen, as a way to get involved in their role, learn more about the character they had to become, and how they could improve their performances on stage or on screen. This technique was interesting because if I could dress the part as others, I could also replicate their behavior and method act as them. My goal was set to method act other people whenever I wasn't currently cast in a theatre production, meaning I would have extra time to do this behaviour. To me, it was a way to practice acting instead of waiting to be cast in a play or musical, I could just act as another person during my normal daily life. Who would be the first person I would mimic down to every detail I could? I had to find a person that nobody else had replicated or even dared to do before to test my method acting ability as extreme as I could.

Not sure about what you do in your free time, but I watch a lot of YouTube. There are all sorts of content creators I enjoy watching, one of them is Jason, or his channel name goes by *VEE3RDEYE*. I remember running into him at a *Warped Tour* festival back in 2014. He had big swoopy hair like I did back in the day, while also wearing skinny jeans, which is something I wore daily as well. It seemed that Jason and I had a similar appearance. Later that day, I found him on YouTube and it seemed he got a wide amount of views because of his unique look. I subscribed to his channel but didn't watch much of his content as time went on. Then this guy disappears, it seems he drops off the face of the planet. Years later he re-emerges on his channel with blue dreadlocks, and he started dressing completely different, dropping the skinny jeans and wearing hippie-like clothing. He published a video talking about how he got addicted to weed edibles and how psychedelics changed his life. To me, I thought his appearance was eye-catching, and his mindset of not wanting to smoke weed and instead choosing to eat edibles due to that method of consumption being a healthier choice for the human body was quite an interesting concept to think about. I was already starting a journey of getting dreadlocks and recently had my whole brain shifted when it came to taking LSD, I figured that Jason would be the very next person that I would replicate in my life. I watched loads of his videos to the point where I could mimic his catchphrases, understand his interests, and even consume weed in a similar fashion. I also changed my online username to veeonepew, which was an old username he used to have for his second Instagram account where he posted various photos from his travels.

Due to my appearance, I of course was able to get the same reactions he got from others, which was attention. Walking around New York City with blue dreadlocks came with its benefits. Many people wanted to take photos of me, users online started to recognize how I looked similar to Jason and would watch my content because of this aspect, and I stood out like a sore thumb with my hair being an easy talking point. It made it easy for people to talk to me because of my appearance. The first phrase that usually came out of their mouth was usually something about my hair. My realization of it being successful was when people started sending me a post on Instagram.

A local big Instagram page called hipsters_of_ny had received a photo somebody took of me standing at Bryant Park's subway station and posted it on their feed with a description of how they thought I would act as a person.

In one way, I felt extremely proud that I could replicate somebody so well with how they look, and on another end, I was a little embarrassed that a lot of my identity was based on somebody else. I replicated Jason because I was in a rough patch with my life, having very little friends in the city, and struggling with my mental health. Copying Jason helped distract me from my own problems for the time being. However, soon I realized that even though the attention was nice, I still struggled to explain to others why I did this. Some people would ask why I dyed my hair blue, and if they didn't know Jason, I could come up with any explanation. To those online who watched *VEE3RDEYE*, they asked why I had a similar username and why I looked exactly like him. It's hard to say that I was in a period of my life where I was confused, had a drug issue, and didn't know who I wanted to be. I thought explaining the full reason as to why I was mimicking somebody would be too dark for people to hear. My replication became a problem because I couldn't depict what was me anymore and what I was simply replicating.

In order to regain control over my life, I started to shift completely away from replication. There were some things I enjoyed from mimicking others that I will keep in my life, however I think small things like my hair color and username could be changed. I soon switched all my online profiles to a different username, moopliss, and dyed my hair blonde. The impact of Doopliss as a character in my life with the combination of the first letter of my name was the origin and birth of this username. It felt good to walk away from looking and feeling like Jason. I realize that we as people get inspired by others with how they look and want to try it out on ourselves. There is nothing wrong with wanting to look or recreate something we like, which is something we all do on holidays like Halloween or any themed parties we attend. The important part is where to draw the line. Replicating somebody to every nook and cranny they have within themselves isn't something I suggest doing. You miss out on being able to show the world who you are as a person, and that's something earth needs more of, individuality. Even though a lot of individuality is inspired from other things, we can pick bits and pieces from other humans to make up a person we like to be. The key is moderation, making sure that we don't mimic and replicate other people entirely, that way you have room to let yourself be you.

Oftentimes it is scary to be your own person. It's why there are countless films and animation movies that teach us this lesson as their morale of the story. They always shout the phrase "Just be yourself" and it's ironic in a way that sometimes being yourself is knowing that you are influenced by others. There are parts of you that are taken from what you see. We can't help doing it either because as humans we are sponges to what we choose to look and pay attention to. Wherever we plant ourselves on this planet, the environment around us will shape who we are. It's why people who believe in certain political views typically don't change their opinions simply due to the fact that the media they consume and the people they follow online say the same statements and beliefs that they do. Maybe there is a time you feel bad in your life because you find yourself having moments where you too are doing exactly what Doopliss does. It's okay. Don't stress too much about it, but if you jump to the part where you are mimicking somebody so much that you are becoming a whole blown Italian plumber named Mario, I suggest stepping back and choosing to make room for the real you to breathe.

Fully Functional Child

There is this area close to where I live called Galgenberg. The translation of this location is kind of weird because it means Gallow Mountain. Back in the day, they would bring people up this area and would hang them due to whatever crimes they had committed. There is only farmland up top since it's away from the city with plenty of open space. My guess is that they brought people up there to kill them because they didn't want the public to openly see people hanging in town. Quite a weird fact to know while climbing this mini mountain every other day whenever I need a break from technology or the indoors. My sandals are broken, which means I've been walking barefoot up this mountain. Occasionally, I step on a rock or two which irritates me, but I am happy to step onto some grass and just stare at the clouds moving slowly along the horizon. Maybe I'm just getting old, and this is what adults do to get their mind off things, but I quite like climbing Death Mountain in my free time. Whatever problems I am dealing with or things that stress me out, I leave them at the bottom of Galgenberg and climb up to the top and enjoy the sights and smells of being outside.

Once I reach the top, sometimes I will find other people roaming around, but as of lately it's been raining with little cold weather, so I've had the top view to myself several times. If I adventure up Galgenberg near the end of the day when the sun is setting, I have an opportunity to see both the sun and the moon at the same time. The first time I saw something like this was when I was on my rooftop in Brooklyn, NY. If you have never wandered outside to try and find the sun and moon showing at the same time, it's quite a sight to see. Once on top of Galgenberg, I stand at the highest point. This is where I look up in the sky and say what I am thankful for in my life. Most things that get listed are my health, the people I love, the fact that I live in a country with no war, and that I am able to walk around and use my body, which is a thing I am happy for and don't take for granted either. This is also the time I tell god to appear, but thus far, he hasn't done anything to show himself, even when I give him the platform and time to do so. The sun goes down, and I can feel the temperature start to change. Cold starts to hit my face and feet, and soon I start to wander back down Death Mountain.

I'd be lying if I said I didn't think about death often. Since I'm alive, the price I have to pay to live is to eventually die. My heart is like the sun. The sun shines down from the sky and allows life to grow on the land, similar to how my heart gives life to me as it pumps blood throughout my body. In the morning, the sun isn't as warm and bright, but then it reaches its full potential when it hits the middle of the day. My body at first isn't strong and mighty, but as time moves on and my heart keeps working, I'm able to grow into a full-sized human. Just like the sun's power fades away as it sets, my body does the same thing as it gets older, and when the sun disappears, I think how my life will reach the same ending.

One day my co-worker talked about how he didn't mind the fact of dying. To be honest, it's kind of a weird statement to hear when somebody mentions that if they died they wouldn't be upset about it. I asked him why because I viewed life with a lot to live for. The interaction with humans, the smell of different places, excitement you get from doing an activity, taste of food, and many other examples. Seems like our planet has a broad range of things to pick and choose from. How on earth can it be okay if death came around the corner?

His answer was that life itself takes effort to stay alive. You must make time to get food for your body, which means you have to go out of your way to find a job, after that you'll have to give up part of your day to acquire this currency, and with whatever time you have left, part of that time should be given towards relationships with others so that you don't feel lonely at the end of the day. The response he gave was depressing to hear, but for many of us, this is our reality. In a way it makes sense that life is difficult to maintain. Many humans don't have perfect health, good money situations, or perhaps their relationships struggle. In order to improve things within our life, we must spend time making it happen. I won't lose weight if I don't use my time by choosing to eat healthy and working out. My co-worker stated he wouldn't head out directly and make an effort to kill himself because he found that life has its good moments, but he stated he wouldn't be sad if tomorrow a bus ran over him. If I told this kind of concept to my parents, they would tell me how life has meaning because god has a plan for me, but no matter how many times I walk up that mountain and ask god to appear, he never does and I can't help but continue being an agnostic atheist. However, just because I don't believe in a god, it doesn't mean I don't find value in living. Waking up and breathing is great because I am allowed to make decisions and go on an adventure each day, regardless of if I have to spend part of my day working to afford to live.

I'm going to be upfront with you, sometimes I wake up and don't feel so confident with my life. Quite frankly, I have absolutely no idea what I am doing at times. Originally, I was going to be a programmer, but then I realized I wanted to act, then I started getting distracted with my goals by using weed and psychedelics, and now I am on this path where I am unsure what I should do next. Perhaps I can keep making content online of things I enjoy, I wish to travel to new areas that I have never been to before, and I also want to grow and make memories with my relationship. The fact that anything can happen tomorrow can be scary but it's also extremely fun and exciting. Life has its twists and turns it throws at you. Once death hits, the story of my life ends and then I can't witness the next page in the book. Words on the paper stop appearing and the only thing I have left is what I made.

Hence, this is the reason why you are reading this book. I wanted to make something that showed what I've been through and what topics are on my mind. I've made numerous mistakes; I've explored a lot of different parts of the planet, but I feel like I've barely scratched the surface of what life has to offer. After some time thinking, my life is like a video game. Blame my parents for putting a controller in my face at a young age, but since life is a choose your own adventure, I realize that it's almost like *Minecraft* or any other open world exploration game. Only rules to follow are the ones that hurt your character if you disobey, like fall damage. If you harm other players, you'll get punished for it. Making the decision to not eat any food will starve your character down to no hearts. Spending time learning and developing a craft can level up your skills, which can allow you to have new paths and opportunities to access in the foreseeable future. Our bodies only have a certain amount of energy per day, meaning we have stats that we have to refill by resting in order to continue doing more within our lifetime. It's hard for me to not associate my life as a giant massively open multiplayer experience, but it's what makes the clearest sense for me.

Does this mean that I am going to run around crazy acting like a total moron because I think life is sort of like a video game? Of course not. You have to realize that we only have one life and that there is no respawn or restart button when it comes to this game. This means that you get to choose what you want to do with your time when you play the game that is your life. Some days when I log into *Guild Wars 2,* I see players who only go and fight giant bosses in hopes of getting shiny rewards. I've run into players who play the game just to talk and hangout in group events, other people sit around at the trading post and simply flip their coins on items in hopes of making more money before they log off for the day. The game has no rules of what you have to be doing, and because of this the game has endless playtime for you until you run out of your own personal goals. It's why many people stop playing big open world games like *World of Warcraft* or *Guild Wars,* they reach a point where their goals they set for themselves are finished, and when it comes time to figuring out the next task to do, they hit a big moment of being clueless on which direction to go.

Currently my life is at this moment where the tinkering of my "life puzzle" is a little bit put together but still unfinished, and I'm not frazzled with what to do next, I think I am just excited to know that I have reached 25 years of age and hopefully have many more years ahead of me. I have put together my opinions of what I think of society, experienced living in different environments, and how I view myself. Living through a pandemic opened my eyes that anything can happen at any moment, and the game I am playing can shift and alter the playing field without any warning. The realization that there are moments where I will say bye to people or activities and that it might be the last time I ever witness those kinds of moments again is crazy to think about. Each time I decide to roll the dice of life, a new outcome comes my way and I'm ready for whatever is around the corner. Maybe in another 25 years I'll write another book on what I have been up to, but as for now, the childhood, teenage, and soon young adult life will sink away into the past. Today I view myself as the smartest and best version of myself. I know that in another year, I'm sure I may look back at this version of myself and will laugh because I understood what I was going through and what awaited me around the horizon.

After my hike up to the top of Galgenberg, my journey back home starts to be lit up by the stars in the sky. With the moon being brightly lit, I realize that it's simply a big rock floating next to the giant rock I currently call home. I remember that I am a tiny living organism that is somehow able to breathe and stay alive in the middle of a giant galaxy of darkness. There are still things that scare me in life, spiders, failure and of course death. Apparently, I also fear the ending of this book because I realize that in a way, my thoughts as a young person end as well. If humans lived forever, there would be too many of us taking up space on earth. Perhaps this is my way of trying to comfort myself that all things do come to an end. Even though I may be 25 years old, the fact I wander around outside with no shoes on, enjoy staying up late even though I have work in the morning, and would have no problem playing video games for hours on end each day, perhaps the inside of me is just a fully functional child. If I take life seriously, it's lame because then I'm uptight and feed my anxiety to stress about the future. Although I partially agree that it's important to prepare for the adult life, which is the normal route of thinking society wants you to take, let me give you a sprinkle of life advice that I live by to this day, if it's normal then it's probably not fun.

If you want to view more from Matthew, you can follow his YouTube, TikTok, Twitch, Instagram and other social media platforms under the username moopliss.

Milton Keynes UK
Ingram Content Group UK Ltd.
UKHW022316131123
432492UK00010B/166